ROBERT DAVIDSON

ROBERT DAVIDSON

EAGLE OF THE DAWN

EDITED BY IAN M. THOM

With essays by Aldona Jonaitis,

Marianne Jones

and Ian M. Thom

University of Washington Press

Seattle

Published in the United States of America by the
University of Washington Press,
P.O. Box 50096, Seattle, WA 98145-5096

Published simultaneously in Canada by
Douglas & McIntyre,
1615 Venables Street,
Vancouver, British Columbia V5L 2H1

Library of Congress Cataloging-in-Publication Data
Davidson, Robert, 1946–
    Robert Davidson : eagle of the dawn / edited by Ian Thom; with essays by
Aldona Jonaitis, Marianne Jones, and Ian Thom.
            p.   cm.
    Includes bibliographical references (p.   ) and index.
    ISBN 0-295-97260-2
    1. Davidson, Robert, 1946–   . 2. Haida Indians—Art. 3. Haida
Indians—Sculpture.   I. Thom, Ian M. II. Jonaitis, Aldona,
1948–   . III. Jones, Marianne. IV. Title V. Title: Eagle of
the dawn.
E99.H2D393   1993   93-30
709'.2—dc20   CIP

Editing by Saeko Usukawa
Design by Barbara Hodgson
Cover photograph: *Gagiit* mask, 1984 (red cedar, human hair, operculum,
    acrylic, feathers). Collection of Joshua I. Latner. *Photo: Louis Joncas*
Back cover photograph: *Raven Bringing Light to the World*, 1983–84
    (yellow cedar, abalone). Private collection. *Photo: Trevor Mills*
Colour separations and printing by Hemlock Printers Ltd.
Binding by North-West Book Co. Ltd.
Text paper: Celesta Dull 100 lb., Westvaco Corporation
Printing inks: Hostmann-Steinberg
Printed and bound in Canada

Published with assistance from the British Columbia Heritage Trust.

Excerpts from *A Haida Potlatch* by Ulli Steltzer, copyright © 1984 by Ulli
Steltzer, appear with the permission of Douglas & McIntyre.

Excerpts from *Robes of Power: Totem Poles on Cloth*, edited by Doreen Jensen
and Polly Sargent, are reprinted with permission of the publisher, University
of British Columbia Press, copyright © 1986 by Kitanmax Northwest Coast
Indian Arts Society. All rights reserved by the publisher.

Captions:
p. ii: *Killer Whale Fin* 1986–87
Yellow cedar
52.9 x 14.7 x 29.5 cm
PRIVATE COLLECTION

p. iii: *Dorsal Fin* 1987
Red cedar, acrylic
188 x 48 x 96 cm
PRIVATE COLLECTION

p. iv: *Robert Davidson in his studio, 1993*
PHOTO BY ULLI STELTZER

Photo Credits

All photographs are by Trevor Mills, except as follows:

Harold Demetzer, 119 (bottom)
Holly Hames: 69
Louis Joncas: front cover, 136, 137
Robert Keziere: 27, 29, 30, 31, 32, 36, 37, 40, 41, 43, 47,
    51, 52, 53, 58, 60, 61, 74 (bottom), 87, 103, 105, 121,
    122, 123, 132, 135, 149
David Milne: 114–15, 119 (top)
Royal British Columbia Museum: 38, 39, 76, 77, 80, 81
Ulli Steltzer, iv, 21, 74 (top), 84, 85, 94, 98
Thunder Bay Art Gallery: 120
Museum of Anthropology, University of British
    Columbia: 42 (bottom), 90

CONTENTS

FOREWORD

by Willard Holmes

This book and the exhibition it documents are a long overdue testament to the role that Robert Davidson has played in the preservation and enrichment of contemporary Haida culture. The Vancouver Art Gallery has had, for a contemporary art museum, a relatively long history of acquiring and exhibiting art of the Northwest Coast indigenous cultures as artworks rather than artifacts. With *Arts of the Raven* in 1967 and the Bill Reid retrospective in 1974, the gallery established itself in the forefront of Western-based institutions willing to address the remarkably complex and difficult issue of contemporary Native cultural forms.

With *Robert Davidson: Eagle of the Dawn*, the gallery is continuing this exploration and commitment. There is perhaps no artist who has contributed as much as Robert Davidson to the culture he draws upon and the community he lives in. Not only in his art but in his commitment to the young of Haida Gwaii, he has walked the often difficult road of a Native artist in a Western world. That he has done so with such a degree of grace and artistic vision is a true sign of the strength of his culture.

There is little doubt that the recent opening up of scholarship and investigation into contemporary Native culture has laid bare many premises of the recent past and revealed their complicity, either knowing or unknowing, with systems which specify a place for Native art, in the spotlight, but always on the periphery. With *Robert Davidson: Eagle of the Dawn*, the Vancouver Art Gallery has recognized the importance and indeed necessity of acknowledging those artists in our midst, no matter what their cultural origins, who have enriched the present by creating a bridge between the past and future. Robert Davidson is exemplary in this instance and deserves our very great thanks.

I would like to express my gratitude to all of the staff at the Vancouver Art Gallery and Douglas & McIntyre who have contributed to making this project such a success. In particular, I would like to thank Scott McIntyre of Douglas & McIntyre, and Ian Thom and Janet Meredith here at the gallery, for the collegiality they showed in bringing the two organizations together to make this project possible. Finally, thanks to all of the lenders, both institutional and private, who consented to part with their works for an extended period of time so that Robert Davidson, the Haida culture and all Native communities can be recognized and appreciated for their ongoing contribution to the evolution of contemporary North American culture.

Willard Holmes
Director, Vancouver Art Gallery

ACKNOWLEDGEMENTS

The funding for the initial research on this project and its realization as a book and exhibition was granted by the Canada Council, and I am grateful to my colleagues who gave me a vote of confidence in supporting the idea. The Stewart Fund has contributed generously to the book. The Vancouver Art Gallery would like to thank Placer Dome Inc. and Fraser Fell in particular for their benevolent sponsorship of this project. The Vancouver showing of the exhibition was graciously supported by Polygon Group Limited. My debt to colleagues at other institutions, Alan Hoover at the Royal British Columbia Museum, Dr. George MacDonald and Sandy Lorimer and the staff at the Canadian Museum of Civilization, is considerable. The staffs of many other organizations—especially the Museum of Anthropology at the University of British Columbia and the Thunder Bay Art Gallery—helped as well. Private collectors, most of whom prefer to remain anonymous, have been more than generous in allowing us access to their works, and to all of them a most sincere thanks.

My fellow essayists, Aldona Jonaitis and Marianne Jones, have been a pleasure to work with, and I salute them both. Lynn Brockington provided invaluable help with the Bibliography, and Robin Laurence compiled the Chronology and List of Exhibitions. The editorial skill of Saeko Usukawa has clarified the prose considerably.

At the Vancouver Art Gallery, I would like to thank the many people who assisted me in this project, especially Nancy Kirkpatrick, Angela Mah, Rosemary Emery, Janet Meredith and Colette Warburton. Other staff members, particularly Amy Algard and June Beatty in registration, were understanding of all the requirements of such a project, and I appreciate their forbearance and skill. Two photographers, Trevor Mills and

Robert Keziere, provided most of the images, and I am grateful to them for their care and exacting standards.

Several of Robert Davidson's dealers have been most helpful. My thanks to Bud Mintz of Potlatch Arts, Derek Simpkins of the Gallery of Tribal Art and Joseph Murphy of the Inuit Gallery of Vancouver for assisting me in locating pieces and often providing information about them.

My greatest thanks go to the artist himself. His unfailing good grace in the face of many, many questions and, of course, the strength of his work have made the project a rewarding and worthwhile one.

Finally, I am grateful to Scott McIntyre, who had faith and made the book possible, and to Barbara Hodgson, who made it beautiful.

Ian M. Thom
Vancouver, 1993

ROBERT DAVIDSON

The Essays

TRADERS OF TRADITION *by Aldona Jonaitis*

THE EVOLUTION OF AN ARTIST *by Ian M. Thom*

G̱UUD SAN GLANS *by Marianne Jones*

Eagle Spirit Mask 1980

Yellow cedar, operculum,

goat hair, brass, acrylic,

eagle feathers

22.8 x 22.3 x 15.5 cm

PRIVATE COLLECTION

TRADERS OF TRADITION

The History of Haida Art

by Aldona Jonaitis

More than family connects Charles Edenshaw, the most renowned Haida artist of the turn of the century, with his great-grandson Robert Davidson.[1] Both are artists of dazzling creativity; both take the conventions of Haida art and transform them into personal aesthetic statements. Splendid talent and innovation characterize both. But something else connects Edenshaw and Davidson—their existence in a world that simultaneously celebrates their achievements and mourns the demise of the cultures that gave those achievements life. Edenshaw created immortal works at a time when Haida culture was said to be dying, while Davidson began carving and painting when Haida culture was thought by many non-Natives to be a thing of the past.

Metaphors of birth, death and rebirth assume a central position in Western literature. The usual description of Haida art history follows a mythic scenario founded on these metaphors: it focusses on the great nineteenth-century florescence of two- and three-dimensional style, describes the demise of that shortly after the death of Charles Edenshaw in 1920, and celebrates a dramatic rebirth in the 1960s, when Bill Reid and Bill Holm rediscovered the forgotten canons of the nineteenth-century northern style. It is time to balance this narrative of retrieving lost heritage that characterizes the representation of the Northwest Coast renaissance by investigating those Haida artistic traditions that persisted throughout the twentieth century and thus did not need revival. As Marcia Crosby has pointed out, we need to reassess the messages behind the concept of the Northwest Coast renaissance to reveal how they misconstrue certain historical realities.[2] To do so, it is first necessary to understand certain central assumptions behind some earlier anthropology—that Native people had, prior to contact, lived in unified, cohesive communities and shared common values; that the inherent perfection of their culture disintegrated as

I can only speak about the Haida culture. It started dying in my great-grand-fathers' generation—Charlie Edenshaw's generation. He knew it was dying, so he spent his whole lifetime carving to carry over. My grand-parents' generation, they were in turmoil because of the two cultures coming together.
—Robert Davidson, interview with Carol Sheehan McLaren, Canadian Conservation Institute, August 1978, Massett, Haida Gwaii

What I try to do is to connect people to the world—through the art.
—Robert Davidson, *The Northwest, a Collector's Vision*, 1986, Barrie Art Gallery

3

the overwhelming forces of the dominant society caused first a decline and then the disappearance of their traditions, including art; that on the northern Northwest Coast in particular, the loss of artistic competence was reversed only when individuals from outside the cultures rediscovered earlier stylistic conventions.[3]

It is noteworthy that a major scholar of the Haida, Margaret Blackman, observed as early as 1976 that there exists "an unacknowledged but nonetheless extant attitude among anthropologists which holds the aboriginal cultures as inherently more worthy of investigation, more interesting, and somehow more 'real' than the cultures which evolved under subsequent culture change."[4] Ignoring acculturation denies Native people their history, and implicitly endorses the fallacy of precontact purity and postcontact contamination.[5] In truth, Native groups had never existed in pristine isolation from each other; on the Northwest Coast, evidence of interaction and mutual influence appears in the archaeological and historical records.[6] Once more distant travellers appeared on the scene, they too interacted with and mutually influenced Native cultures.[7] Blackman comments how "despite earlier pronouncements of the decline of Northwest Coast ceremonialism in the first half of the 20th century,"[8] a considerable number of traditions persisted in contemporary Northwest Coast ceremonials.[9]

As well as identifying the continuity of past traditions, we must accept the validity of newly invented traditions as legitimate expressions of a Native presence in the contemporary world. This is not merely an academic question; narratives that announced the death, or at least the disintegration, of Native cultures contributed to their disempowerment by segregating them into timeless "Others" unable to accommodate creatively and with strength to new and often difficult circumstances.[10] Moreover, by depicting Native peoples as succumbing to the forces of acculturation, such representations implicitly granted the dominant society a cultural hegemony over those it colonized.[11]

Recent scholarship has begun to dispute such images of total cultural destruction; as Guy Brett puts it, "Another outcome of the resurgence of the Third World has been to reveal unmistakably that peoples responded to colonialism not as passive victims but as active subjects, making their own representation of the experience from their point of view, as part of a survival struggle." [12] The discourse of colonialism, with its message of deteriorating cultural presences that situates the dominant society in a superior and victorious position has, happily, begun to be dismantled, to be replaced by a more liberating discourse of postcolonial cultural endurance in the global community. It is from this perspective that I discuss some moments in Haida art history in order to demonstrate how art made for sale to outsiders speaks insistently and eloquently of cultural endurance. [13]

———————————

The tragic realities of Haida history make them prime subjects for a narrative of disappearance; in this representation, they plummet from the height of cultural achievement to virtually nothing. Prior to first contacts with non-Natives at the end of the eighteenth century, the Haida had a population estimated at over 14,000. [14] Early trade of sea otter furs with European and American sailing vessels infused wealth, metal tools, and an even greater cosmopolitanism than before, resulting, among other things, in a flourishing of ceremonialism, new construction in villages, and the proliferation of exquisitely carved totem poles. Even when the seaborne trade declined after 1810, the Haida persisted in their trading activities with the Hudson's Bay Company posts established at Fort Simpson on the mainland in 1831, at Victoria in 1843, and at Massett in 1869. [15]

Haida art of this period has assumed a privileged place within the literature on the Northwest Coast. A visit to Haida Gwaii (the Queen Charlotte Islands) in 1791 inspired the Frenchman Etienne Marchand to write about "the execution of [an art] which bespoke a taste and perfection which we do not expect to find in countries where the men seem still to have the appearance of savages. But what must astonish most, . . . is to see painting everywhere, everywhere sculpture, among a nation of hunters." [16] In 1881, Norwegian-born Adrian Jacobsen visited the Haida on a collecting expedition for the Royal Berlin Ethnological Museum and described totem poles "that no tribe on the mainland can produce . . . I found that the poles of the Haida are painted in brighter colours than those on the mainland. Another difference between these groups is that the Haida poles, although older, are more beautiful and more artistically developed." [17]

I like the idea that you have an understanding of how it used to be, or how it's done. And then you can be creative and innovative and inventive.
—Robert Davidson, interview with Carol Sheehan McLaren, Canadian Conservation Institute, August 1978, Massett, Haida Gwaii

He started to innovate, and that makes it different. His drawing, his different colours, his design, his ideas . . . what he does is always good. Good craftsmanship is one of the trademarks of our art, and he's a great craftsman.
—James Hart, Haida artist, interview with Ian Thom, July 1992

Over a hundred years later, Bill Holm had great praise for this art: "Haida artists worked in every medium available on their islands as well as those they were obliged to import, and their production was widely admired and desired. They built the most monumental houses, the largest and the greatest number of totem poles, the grandest canoes, as well as some of the most elegant and refined bowls, chests, and masks."[18]

A devastating smallpox epidemic in 1862 decimated the Haida, whose population declined so precipitously that by 1880 only two native villages on Haida Gwaii remained inhabited. The other towns stood unoccupied, their surviving residents having relocated to Skidegate and Massett.[19] By 1915, the 588 remaining Haida had converted to Christianity, learned English, ceased potlatching, and sold much of their ceremonial regalia to the ever-willing museum collectors.[20]

Anthropologist John Swanton visited Haida Gwaii from fall 1900 to spring 1901, as a member of the American Museum of Natural History's Jesup North Pacific Expedition.[21] He wrote sad letters to his mentor in New York, Franz Boas, detailing what he perceived as the utter destruction of a once-proud people. On 30 September 1900, Swanton wrote Boas that the missionaries were largely to blame, having suppressed the old dances and encouraged the abandonment of the old houses; they had, Swanton said, destroyed "everything that makes life worth living."[22] It is only in this correspondence that Swanton described what he encountered on Haida Gwaii; his publications contain no mention of what turn-of-the-century Massett or Skidegate were actually like. Informed by the ethos of "salvage" anthropology based upon the premise that the real subject of ethnographic research was precontact culture, Swanton's monograph[23] aims at reconstructing how the Haida lived before the 1860s.[24]

For much of the twentieth century, descriptions of the Haida followed suit with narratives of destruction and despair, such as that provided by Carol Sheehan in her introduction to a book on Haida argillite sculpture:

When the rush of foreign influences subsided, Northwest Coast culture had been radically altered. The magnificent monuments in cedar, the totem poles unique to the coast, became relics of a past and dying culture. The elaborate and extravagant community feasts or potlatches that marked the totem-pole raisings and the attendant public proclamations of individual social and spiritual advancement were no longer celebrated. The laws and religious practices of the strangers, bland by comparison with these native traditions, were adopted. The great feast houses were replaced by prim Victorian houses with gingerbread gables. The songs, stories and other long-held beliefs began to fade, as did the native languages, with the ubiquitous spread of Christianity and the prosperity promised in its irresistible new ethic.[25]

There is no question that the forces of colonialism were extremely destructive, and as a result of contact with non-Natives, the Haida endured a large-scale transformation of their culture. It is nonetheless also true that Swanton chose to ignore the means by which the Haida accommodated to the forces of change resulting from contact with the dominant culture. As Blackman reminds us, "creativity in acculturation" exists to balance the hopeless picture of social decay which has persisted until very recently.[26] Among the Haida, tombstones replaced totem poles as mortuary memorials, and reciprocal feasting replicated the social functions of the potlatch.[27] There was also the case of argillite.

As early as the 1820s, some Haida began a commercial venture which continues to the present as they began to offer for sale sculptures of argillite, a carbonaceous shale. Throughout the nineteenth century, travellers to Native communities in the United States and Canada delighted in purchasing a memento of their visit, and voyagers to Haida Gwaii were no exception. By the 1880s, many steamers that plied the coast visited Skidegate Inlet where tourists could purchase the "curiosities" which, according to Jacobsen, were very expensive.[28]

Thanks to the meticulous scholarship of Bill Holm, Robin Wright, Peter Macnair, Alan Hoover and others, we have an excellent history of nineteenth-century argillite carving. The earliest carvings for sale included pipes with designs derived from Haida style, as well as those depicting foreign ships, white men and women, Western-style houses and even horses. Then came figures of white people, copies of the small wooden bowls used to hold eulachon grease, as well as European-style plates and

I was concerned about how to do it, how to bring myself to that level in order to push myself. Another thing you have to be aware of is the level that all those artists attained during the 1850s, and once I am able to attain that level, I feel that I can go in my own direction. Because each artist in that period went in their own direction, and yet it was a style of that period. And yet each one, if you look at it, went in different directions.
—Robert Davidson, interview with Carol Sheehan McLaren, Canadian Conservation Institute, August 1978, Massett, Haida Gwaii

7

platters. By the middle of the century, model totem poles assumed a central position in the argillite repertoire, where they have remained until the present. By the 1880s, carvers had turned away from non-Native imagery and created a wealth of sculptures including model chests, figures and figure groups, as well as plates and pipes with distinctly Haida motifs, much of it in the narrative style so typical of this genre.[29]

Over the past century, opinions on the value of argillite have been divided. In the 1890s, Major J. W. Powell of the Bureau of American Ethnology, for example, rejected argillite carvings in principle as they were "designed for sale to the higher race [and] . . . in no proper sense represent Indian arts."[30] By omitting any illustration of argillite in the section on "The Representation of the Crest and of Myth in Art" in his classic "Contributions to the Ethnology of the Haida,"[31] John Swanton overlooked a wealth of material that contained compelling images of both crests and myth (although he did use model totem poles and houses).[32]

Later in the twentieth century, Wolfgang Paalen, a surrealist artist fascinated by the Northwest Coast, made the following assessment of argillite:

> I have not reproduced any objects [of argillite] because, although at times beautiful and of great craftsmanly perfection, they represent only the decadent stage at which a great art loses its raison d'être and degenerates to trifles. For this art was so integral a part of indigenous life that it could not survive the destruction of the social organization from which it sprang. . . . To limit the creative power of these people to petty decorative tasks, and to confound the products of the souvenir market with their authentic expressions merely degrades their great art which was of entirely collective purpose: an art for consummation and not for individual possession.[33]

Others have responded more positively to argillite. In the catalogue of the Museum of Modern Art's historic 1941 exhibition, *Indian Art of the United States,* Frederic H. Douglas and Rene d'Harnoncourt comment on how rapidly this nontraditional art achieved a high level of perfection, possibly because wood carving had already been so firmly established among the Haida.[34] In 1953, Marius Barbeau published the first book solely devoted to this medium, *Haida Myths Illustrated in Argillite Carvings*, followed four years later by *Haida Carvers in Argillite*.[35] In the introduction to the 1957 publication, Barbeau had the following glowing words for argillite:

> The arrival of the white man in Alaska and on the North Pacific Coast after 1741 . . . did not smother the vitality and activities of the Mongolian-like tribes of this area, as it is generally believed, nor blunt their skills and handicrafts. Far from it! . . . [out of these contacts] evolved a craftsmanship and an art that are well-nigh unsurpassed in North America, if not elsewhere as well. Let this book draw out of a deceptive obscurity the notable works of Haida carvers in argillite, most of whom were thriving in the second half of the nineteenth century! Their contribution to culture at large will eventually find its way into the forums of universality.[36]

Virtually all publications specifically about argillite as well as those including these carvings in overviews of Northwest Coast art admit to its commercial origins but concentrate on its adherence to the Haida canon. Northwest Coast art surveys such as *Arts of the Raven*, *The Legacy*, *Box of Daylight*, *Spirit and Ancestor* and *From the Land of the Totem Poles*, among others, include argillite unapologetically alongside other examples of Haida art.[37]

Haida argillite carving presents a fascinating problem for the student of Northwest Coast art. As Ruth Phillips has demonstrated, curios made for sale to non-Natives often assume a low position within the hierarchy of Native art.[38] Thus, because it was made for sale and had for much of the nineteenth century been a favourite souvenir of ship captains and tourists, argillite could suffer from the label "tourist art." However, because it displays the sophisticated formline style characteristic of northern Northwest Coast art, it could just as easily be classified with the best pieces made for use within the community;[39] this gives it a stature not often granted art made for the non-Native market.[40] Nonetheless, one still must ask whether its commoditization—the transformation of a thing into a commodity to be exchanged—renders it somehow less authentic than the art intended to be used within the community.[41]

I think that the person who really revived argillite carving was Marius Barbeau when he came out with that book. He had tons of illustrations of argillite totem poles and that really inspired the people here in Skidegate to start carving again and I was one of them. I used to copy a lot of the totem poles in the book . . . from the book. And then my knowledge of their work accelerated when I met Bill Reid. That is when I started seeing beyond. I started learning a lot more about the culture, the art.
—Robert Davidson, interview with Carol Sheehan McLaren, Canadian Conservation Institute, August 1978, Massett, Haida Gwaii

Ceremony plays a very important role in culture.
—Robert Davidson, comment at the publication of the book *Bill Reid*, April 1986, University of British Columbia Museum of Anthropology

Wolfgang Paalen was not alone in his view that Native art must fit securely into a harmonious and integrated culture and that once artists enter the mainstream of the modern world, their creations become tainted, polluted and not really real.[42] Certainly carvings made as commodities fly in the face of any notion of artistic purity. One can interpret this romanticizing concept of "the genuine Indian making authentic Indian art" as satisfying some deep-seated desire on the part of non-Natives to return to a more unified moment denied them by the complexities of the modern world.[43] The "yearning for singularization" that Igor Kopytoff identifies, similar to the "longing" central to Susan Stewart's analysis of collecting, Renato Rosaldo's "imperialist nostalgia" and Nicholas Thomas's "ideology of primitivism," in part inspires members of modern capitalist society to impose values of stability, unchangeability, and "tradition" upon non-Western cultures.[44]

The literature that positively evaluates argillite acknowledges but does not dwell upon its commercial origin and focusses instead on how this art embodies that elusive thing, "tradition." Those who like Paalen dismiss argillite assert that because it was made for sale, it has no aura of authenticity, regardless of what it looks like.[45] As Walter Benjamin noted, a mediaeval Madonna was not, at the time of its creation, identified as "authentic"; it only became considered so in subsequent centuries.[46] One wonders whether the Haida carvers who knew their stunning creations were to leave their villages for points elsewhere concerned themselves with whether they were making genuine Haida art. The issue of authenticity becomes far more relevant for those who study, purchase and exhibit this art than for those who created it. One way to look at this issue is to contrast the authenticity of the style of Haida argillite sculpture with what we might characterize as its inauthenticity of function.[47]

At the very time that the Haida were said to be losing their traditions—from the 1880s to the first decades of the twentieth century—one of the most creative artists anywhere was working on Haida Gwaii. Charles Edenshaw has been recognized for some time as the master of his genre: unique, original and distinctive. Franz Boas, who worked with him in

1897, identified Edenshaw at one point as "one of the most famous artists of the Haida" and later as "the best carver and painter . . . among the Haida."[48] Bill Holm describes Edenshaw as a master of his tradition "who had developed a very personal version of that tradition,"[49] while Peter Macnair comments that "because of its innovative qualities, it is difficult to compare [Edenshaw's] work with that of his contemporaries and even with that of his traditional forebears"; these creations embody "a vigour and personality seldom found [on art] made by most other artists."[50]

Edenshaw has the notable distinction of being the only Native artist identified by name five times in Boas's classic *Primitive Art*. At a time when most Native peoples found their way into the literature as anonymous informants, this is an outstanding and well deserved acknowledgement of his forceful artistic presence.[51] However, one must not forget that other artists of note were working at the same time. Although a genius, Edenshaw (like other geniuses) was not isolated. Thanks to the meticulous scholarship that has characterized much of the research on Haida art, we know the names of some of his superb colleagues, such as Gwaytihl, John Robson, John Cross and Tom Price, and can identify the hands of other artists such as the Master of the Chicago Settee.[52]

The artists of this generation sold their creations not only to tourists but to museum professionals as well. In addition to masks, headdresses and rattles, Gwaytihl created for sale some shaman figures which ended up in museum collections as representations of an extinct practice.[53] John Robson carved model totem poles for John Swanton, drew crest figures for Charles Newcombe, and created two house models, one currently in the Field Museum, the other in the Canadian Museum of Civilization.[54] Although Edenshaw made art for use within his community, he also drew crest and mythological figures for Boas, explained for him designs on artifacts, and, in response to Swanton's commission, created model poles and houses for the collection of the American Museum of Natural History.[55]

The creation of art on commission for ethnographers and museums suggests an additional dimension which has ramifications for our understanding the history of Haida art—the movement of argillite out of Haida Gwaii and directly into museums. Like the argillite carvings of their predecessors, the creations of Edenshaw and his generation began to circulate in the larger world community. While most earlier argillite had been

I started to go to museums and saw for the first time art beyond my wildest dreams, done by my ancestors, art I could not relate to, art whose purpose I did not know. I saw photographs of these ancient villages, with many totem poles lining the fronts of the villages. I was in dreamland. I was in the spirit world, images were alive, it was a déjà vu. I had been there before. Where I came from, there was not one piece of evidence that we were once a thriving, rich, and developing people. These images made me hungry. I wanted to learn more about them, what they meant and what they represented. What I got, in retrospect, was second-hand knowledge. I spent many hours studying these new-found treasures and information.

—Robert Davidson,
20 October 1991,
New York

initially purchased by travellers and traders and only later ended up in museums, many of these later works were intended for scientific use. Certainly the anthropologists who commissioned these works believed them to be scientifically valid, even if they were not the more desirable old pieces favoured by collectors.[56]

Thus far I have argued that Haida art did not stop when the forces of acculturation led to the creation of new types of sculpture. Similarly, the history of argillite artworks themselves did not end when they were purchased and left Haida Gwaii. Just as the static positioning of Native people in a golden age without history is no longer acceptable, their cultural products can no longer be seen as ahistoric and timeless. In previous publications, I employed the idea of "wrapping" to show how once an artifact leaves its originating community, it is subject to various representations such as publication and museum exhibition; these representations wrap the artifact with new meanings that resonate with the artifact itself, creating a dynamic, ever-changing document of past, present and, ultimately, future significance.[57] Understood this way, the history of Haida art includes the literature which describes and analyses it, the museum exhibitions that display it, and what the contemporary Haida think about it.[58]

Because Haida carvers intended argillite to be sold and removed from their communities, we can also consider its movements beyond Haida Gwaii to constitute another form of wrapping. Drawing upon the post-colonial critics such as Homi Bhabha and Edward Said, Kevin Robins urges scholars to analyse cultural products within the context of a globalization which confronts the no longer acceptable yearnings for a pristine primitivism.[59] Similarly, as James Clifford reminds us, by concentrating upon the integrated group unsullied by contacts with the outside world, anthropology has ignored the very real external connections of that group. He proposes a new focus on "travelling cultures" to investigate their external connections.[60] By analysing the kind of commoditization they underwent, subtle differences can be discerned between the external connections of the pre-Edenshaw argillite and those of works by Edenshaw and his generation. After Edenshaw made his models and drew his formline designs for Boas and Swanton, they became museum artifacts, where they joined numerous other earlier argillite works that had been made as tourist items (whether or not it was tourists or museum collectors who actually purchased them).

Unlike the earlier argillite which became museum specimens by metamorphosis (that is, they were not originally intended as such in their production as items to trade to visitors), Edenshaw's turn-of-the-century commissions were museum specimens by *destination*.[61] Circulating out of the community and without diversion into private hands, these creations landed in institutions which used them to represent cultures that, if not gone, were about to go. When the first ship captains purchased their argillite curios, they had no interest (or so it would appear) that the culture of the sellers was about to be drastically transformed. Similarly, when the tourists purchased their souvenirs either on Haida Gwaii or in shops in Vancouver or Victoria, they may or may not have been much concerned with the fate of the Haida themselves. The situation was quite different for museum commissions.

At the turn of the century, when Boas, Swanton and others were assembling the great museum collections, the prevailing consciousness was of imminent cultural demise. With the best of wills and the noblest of intentions, Franz Boas and his associates genuinely believed in their mission to save for posterity whatever they could of those vanishing cultures. It could be that the sense of loss inherent in the project of salvage anthropology became transferred to the artworks commissioned for that project. As Macnair notes of Edenshaw's works, "the onerous task of leaving a testimony to the past and a legacy for the future surely weighed heavily on him. The flowering of his art perhaps reflects the intensity of his feeling of loss."[62] Although time has obscured whether or not Edenshaw intended such an aura of despair, gloom seems to have become part of his creations once they arrived in the museum. There, positioned among other artifacts, Edenshaw's carvings contributed to a magnificent picture of a culture whose creativity and vitality had become a thing of the past.

Edenshaw and his contemporaries created what has generally been held as the last expressions of the great Haida artistic tradition. Although a number of artists continued to work between the 1920s and the 1960s, virtually all the literature which mentions Haida art made during this time dismisses its validity. Wilson Duff describes the artform as "at a low ebb," with carvers making poles and other items to be sold in urban craft

We are very proud of what our young people are doing. What we all wish for is that they will keep up the tradition. It is very important. All us older people get together and discuss it. There's been such a big long gap in between, more than fifty years, I guess, but now they're starting to revive the culture. It makes us feel so good.
—Henry Geddes,
Haida elder, interview
with Ian Thom,
July 1992

13

*It is becoming our
responsibility to carry on,
creating new paths of
understanding and
solutions in our new
universe, with the cultural
knowledge that has sur-
vived, in the same way our
forefathers created their
own ideas of survival from
their forefathers.*
—Robert Davidson,
18 April 1992

*The Edenshaw memorial
longhouse is a good
design. Robert added a
couple of parts to the
design to make it work
with the shape, and then I
realized he is pretty good.
He worked it all out
design-wise, and it looks
good. You really notice it
when you look at the
original design, when you
see where he made the
variations, but it was all
within the same theme,
the same tradition. It
looks like it's been there
forever.*
—James Hart, Haida
artist, interview with
Ian Thom, July 1992

shops.[63] Macnair comments that carvers lost a "true comprehension of the art,"[64] as older artists failed to pass on their knowledge of form and style, and that work for the predominantly curio market ranged from stiff, although "relatively accomplished" pieces, to "clumsy and crude."[65] Similarly, Sheehan characterizes this art as having "reached a low point, becoming more of a folk art than the highly charged form of expression it had been since its inception a hundred years earlier."[66] Alan Hoover, in his critique of Drew and Wilson's *Argillite: Art of the Haida*, reprimands the authors for promoting indiscriminately the works of more recent carvers: "Although they are unquestionably sincere in their wish to present argillite carving as an important aspect of Haida artistic activity, they do the good name of the tradition a disservice by ignoring the degeneracy that occurred during the early part of the twentieth century."[67]

I cannot, of course, argue for the adherence of this art to the classic Haida formline style, for it clearly did not. Instead, I wish to draw attention to the discourse, which is in many ways far more revealing of the values of the authors than of any intrinsic merits of the art itself. This literature concentrates on what was lost, rather than focussing on the actual production of art during this period. Although acculturated by most external standards, the artists persisted in making an artform which, aesthetically inferior or not, adheres to a particularly Haida tradition of selling art to strangers—for money.

One of the challenges of contemporary anthropology and art history is to seek understanding of the active and affirmative responses that cultures make to their historical conditions in the modern world, and to deconstruct consciously our past biases which blinded us to those Native initiatives. What is of greater relevance to the history of Haida art: that the formline style faded for a time to the background, or that some carvers—even if just a few—continued making art? How significant is it that these carvers created pieces for the curio market? How different in nature is this twentieth-century activity from the nineteenth-century efforts of artists who made pipes replete with ship captains, Western-style houses and horses? How completely tied to a notion of authenticity is the continued narrative of despair that characterizes the comments about post-Edenshaw, pre-Davidson Haida argillite art?

Haida argillite, finally, definitively a commodity, has now arrived at the position of other tourist art, which, because it does not adhere to a canon, is not properly traditional. But what is Haida tradition anyway? I earlier described the internal contradiction between authenticity of style and inauthenticity of function of Haida argillite; this contradiction may be more imaginary than real. In the 1820s, Haida artists realized that the manufacture of carved slate for sale to outsiders was a worthwhile endeavour with certain financial rewards. The abundance of argillite carving produced in the nineteenth century testifies to the cultural value it had for the Haida. Perhaps we should expand the definition of "traditional Haida art" by including that intentionally made for sale. The Haida shared with their neighbours a long-standing tradition of trade. While evidence of pre-contact trade with other Native groups exists, we cannot be certain that they made what we would today call art for movement beyond Haida Gwaii. Certainly by the nineteenth century, the Haida were travelling to the British Columbia mainland to trade their canoes and boxes for, among other items, eulachon grease. And, of course, from their earliest contact with white fur traders, the Haida had exchanged carvings as well as pelts for desirable European and American commodities.

The enthusiasm with which the Haida greeted the market for argillite carvings as well as portrait masks was perhaps partially a reflection of their willingness to produce artworks that were also commodities. As Boas noted in 1888, "The Haida . . . frequently took up foreign ideas with great energy, and developed them independently. . . . It appears that the tribe has a remarkable faculty of adaptation."[68] One manifestation of this adaptability was clearly their participation in an international art market. The crude argillite pieces created between the 1920s and the 1960s can thus signify not so much a degeneration but instead a version of a long-standing tradition. Instead of mourning the loss of a canon (which would soon be reinstated anyway), we should acknowledge the persistence of a tradition.[69] This puts a different, brighter light on the narrative of despair.

––––––––––

Robert Davidson, great-grandson of Charles Edenshaw, was born in Hydaburg, Alaska, in 1946. When he was quite young, his father, Claude Davidson, urged his son to start carving, thus continuing a family tradition

I feel that too much emphasis is placed on ethnology or anthropology and not enough credit given for artistic merit. I think a lot of it is due to the lack of knowledge and lack of acceptance of it as art, but that's changing.
—Robert Davidson, *The Northwest, a Collector's Vision*, 1986, Barrie Art Gallery

I appreciate any—even unfinished—pieces, because you always learn something from them. Robert's skills are very educational, very inspiring in the way of creativity.
—John Yeltatzie, Haida artist, interview with Ian Thom, July 1992

15

that included not only the great Edenshaw but Claude Davidson himself and his father, Robert Davidson Sr. As a result of this encouragement, Robert Davidson began making the small wooden and argillite totem poles like those still being produced on Haida Gwaii. In 1965, Davidson went to Vancouver to complete high school. There he visited museums that displayed some of his ancestors' masterpieces, met Bill Reid and Bill Holm whose guidance helped him perfect his northern-style technique, and seriously began his career as a Haida artist. By the 1970s he was considered the master of an innovative Haida style, and in 1993 became only the second Northwest Coast artist to have a one-person exhibition at a major art gallery.[70]

The northern Northwest Coast renaissance is imbricated in the story of Davidson's development. During the 1960s, the canons of nineteenth-century Haida art had found their way back into the repertoire, in part due to the activities of Bill Reid, who had studied its meticulous formline creations and deciphered its profound underlying aesthetic logic.[71] Concurrently, museum professionals such as Wilson Duff and non-Native artists such as Bill Holm were becoming increasingly smitten with Northwest Coast art, and began to share their admiration with the public by means of exhibitions and publications.[72] Bill Holm's *Northwest Coast Indian Art: An Analysis of Form*[73] justly merits its position as a classic for its meticulous and clear examination of the principles of the exquisite northern style. The confluence of Reid's creative endeavours with Holm's scholarship, the efforts of interested museum professionals, the activities of other Native artists, and the wider attention being paid to the earlier art of his ancestors, inspired the Haida component of what is commonly referred to as the Northwest Coast artistic renaissance.[74]

The representation of Robert Davidson as a major beneficiary of this renaissance—true as that is—downplays his deep artistic roots in Haida Gwaii. In fact, local artists played significant roles in his early development, "because they were all I knew about Haida art when I was growing up."[75] Indeed, Davidson insists that the most significant influences upon his artistic development were his father and grandfather.[76] Davidson speaks with respect and admiration for the artistic achievements of his distinguished grandfather, who in his early days worked with Edenshaw. In 1908, Robert Davidson Sr. and his brother Alfred carved a canoe that

Edenshaw painted; this canoe is currently in the collection of the Canadian Museum of Civilization in Ottawa.[77] Then in 1937, Robert Sr. and Alfred Davidson carved another canoe that Florence Edenshaw Davidson, Robert Sr.'s wife, painted.[78] This tradition of canoe carving continued as late as 1969, when Victor Adams made yet another canoe.

The grandson and grandfather spent long hours together, the young artist receiving quiet inspiration for his developing creativity and appreciation for his Haida heritage. One particularly moving recollection Robert Davidson has is the story of how, in the early 1950s, his grandfather had obtained a loan from the credit union to replace a house destroyed by fire. To pay off this loan, Davidson gave the credit union a collection of argillite totem poles. Robert Davidson describes how seeing this collection, which still is on display in the Kain Credit Union in Prince Rupert, brought tears to his eyes. Davidson insists that growing up in this family, where the grandfather and father carved, provided him with the most important lessons he needed to become a true artist.

Another inspiration for the young Davidson was his great-grandfather Charles Edenshaw, whose memory created a quiet presence. His grandmother Florence Edenshaw Davidson owned some late, comparatively unrefined pieces, which, although made at a time when Edenshaw's hands had become weak, had for Davidson a vitality and strength that would later come to characterize his own art. Davidson also studied the illustrations of Edenshaw's carvings published in *Haida Carvers in Argillite* by Marius Barbeau.[79] These spoke an optimistic message to the young artist that challenged the narrative of despair sometimes applied to Edenshaw's works: "To me, he was chuckling all the time. When I look at his works, there's so much joy in them. He wasn't happy just stacking figures on top of one another. His works were incredibly advanced. He didn't stop at knowing about a form, he kept on developing, never stopping, always experimenting. Edenshaw kept pushing the boundaries of flat design, and anything he did he brought life to."

Davidson recognized early on that other older carvers of Haida Gwaii had individual carving styles. He mentions John Marks, who learned the art of silverwork from Edenshaw; Bill Reid's grandfather Charles Gladstone, who inherited some of Edenshaw's tools; also Moses Ingram, Louis Collison, Tim Pearson, and, especially, Capt. Andrew Brown. Unlike those

Art is a gift from the spirit world. We all have the ability to visualize: that is our connection to the spirit world. When we crystallize these ideas— that is, bring them into this world—we are giving birth to new images, new ideas, and new directions. This can only come from knowledge and experience. Then we are truly living on that edge of the knife. We are now giving new meaning to the songs, dances, crests, and philosophies. We are updating these ideas, which is no different from what our forefathers did.
—Robert Davidson,
20 October 1991,
New York

17

who dismiss the entire generation, Davidson discerned positive qualities in some of this art; the works of Brown, for example, while lacking understanding of formlines and traditional eye forms, "had soul even if they were crude."

A major inspiration for Davidson was Pat McGuire of Skidegate, a quiet man who, despite his lack of formal training, understood the formline tradition. Davidson had heard of McGuire from collectors who praised his exceptional artistry. Wanting to learn more about Haida art, the young man visited McGuire, whose argillite sculpture impressed him with its finesse, unique style, refined sense of design and elegant proportions.[80] They met several times in Vancouver. As both men were not especially talkative, a comfortable silence characterized their interactions. But because art is a visual rather than verbal medium, that did not seem to matter much, as McGuire revealed to Davidson depths of creative possibilities that would contribute to his own outstanding aesthetic development.

Like his ancestors, Davidson creates art both for his community and for sale, not distinguishing between the works he makes for chiefs and for collectors. By masterfully uniting elements of his Haida heritage with the unique needs of the patron, he responds with thoughtfulness and sensitivity to all requests. Certainly when he creates an item of regalia for a potlatch, Davidson balances the formal innovation so characteristic of his style with the requirements of appropriate imagery. For non-Natives, too, he is attentive to the fit of his creation with its ultimate owner. For example, when a Toronto land developer asked for a carving, Davidson thought that the story of Raven bringing the house to the Haida would be suitable for a man who brings houses to his people. Ever eager to discover new visions within his artistic traditions, Davidson describes how he had earlier visited Ninstints, where the compelling moss-enshrouded remains of the internal supports of old Haida houses impressed him with their silent strength. The juncture of ancient ruins and an old legend with new buildings and a metropolitan context inspired Davidson to create for the developer a sculpture depicting the "skeleton" of a house, with centre pole, gable beams and corner posts. The story of Raven bringing houses to the Haida appears on the centre pole, which depicts a Beaver, a Raven transforming into a human, a Frog and a Watchman; two other Watchmen appear on the corner posts.[81]

FACING PAGE:
Bear, Raven and Eagle
Model Pole 1968
Argillite
16.7 x 5.5 x 6 cm
PRIVATE COLLECTION

19

Always pushing himself to the limits of his creativity, Davidson credits participating in ceremonialism, learning to sing, and studying his language as profound enhancements to his continued understanding of Haida art. For example, prior to his 1981 potlatch,[82] he had been more comfortable making prints than painting. Despite this, he decided to distribute decorated drums at that ceremony, thus forcing himself to experiment with colour and formlines in painting. This process, he believes, ultimately accelerated his creativity in the print medium. Before he started singing, he had made masks solely for hanging on walls; now, because he uses so many of his creations in a ceremonial context, he makes certain that all his masks, even those not intended for use, contain functional mouthpieces and can fit comfortably on one's face. And recently, he has devoted himself to learning Haida, because "there are so many ideas and philosophies and beliefs that come through the language." Art introduced Davidson to ceremonialism and singing; these practices consequently motivated him to study his language. This in turn inspired him to new artistry, new innovations.

As the wealth of argillite clearly demonstrates, the nineteenth-century Haida excelled at artistic inventiveness; Davidson maintains this noteworthy tradition. In 1980, he carved an eerie red *Eagle Spirit* mask *(page 2)* so powerful that he hid it away for a year, showing it only to trusted friends. It appeared publicly only after a tragedy devastated him. In 1981, an arsonist destroyed the monument to Charles Edenshaw that Davidson had made with the assistance of eight apprentices: a house in Massett decorated with a carved and painted image of a Frog inspired by a chief's seat by Edenshaw.[83] In despair, Davidson quietly "sang a crying song to the building and saw the image of a burnt frog." He asked his brother Reg to carve a mask of that burnt frog so that at his potlatch, scheduled for later that year, he could properly end his mourning for the house. Davidson did so after the *Frog* mask had appeared in a dance during the first day of his potlatch. At a private ceremony that evening, attended by friends, Davidson placed the mask in a bonfire while everyone sang and drummed. Then Joe David sang a song; at his last drumbeat, the mask disintegrated into the flames. The red *Eagle Spirit* mask, which Davidson realized embodied a vigour and spirit that complemented the grief of the burnt frog, emerged from hiding to be worn by Joe David during a dance at this potlatch. As Davidson describes it, "By burning the *Frog* mask, we acknowledged the destruction of the longhouse with its Frog painting and marked the ending of our mourning for its loss. By dancing with that *Eagle Spirit* mask, we symbolized the life and vitality that balanced the loss of the longhouse."

Having become "a symbol of love we have for ourselves and the strength we need to regain our position in this world," this red *Eagle Spirit* mask remains a part of the regalia of the Rainbow Creek Dancers, a group of Haida performers that includes Robert Davidson and Dorothy Grant. The red *Eagle Spirit* mask takes a privileged place among other newly created masks including a *Salmon (page 138)*, a *Shark (page 118)*, and an *Eagle Transforming into Itself (pages 136 and 137)*. Today, the Rainbow Creek Dancers wear these masks at Haida totem-pole raisings, potlatches and clan ceremonials; potlatches of friends from other Native groups, such as Nuu-chah-nulth artist Joe David; meetings of Native elders and large-scale Native dance festivals, such as the Sealaska-sponsored Celebration '92 held in Juneau, Alaska, as well as at non-Native events throughout Canada and the United States.[84] Like the argillite carvings of his ancestors, Davidson's new creations circulate comfortably in the international arena, continually reinforcing the endurance of the Haida. As he puts it, "We dance in public because that's one way of telling the world we're alive."[85]

Davidson wearing Eagle Transforming into Itself *mask, 1990.* PHOTO BY ULLI STELTZER

In my introduction, I characterized briefly the discourse on Haida art history as a version of a birth-death-rebirth myth; let me refine this somewhat to include some of the underlying assumptions of timelessness and purity, as well as authenticity of style and function that have until recently permeated the evaluation of the Haida artistic tradition. Nineteenth-century Haida art held (and still holds) a privileged position in the literature on Northwest Coast native art. Its luxuriousness, abundance and refinement places it at so high a position of aesthetic excellence that virtually any modification could be considered a degeneration. The argillite carvings of anonymous nineteenth-century masters as well as those of Edenshaw and his contemporaries lend a slightly ambiguous note to this narrative in that

*I don't think of tradition
any more. It's like you
become tradition. Artists
are tradition.*
—Robert Davidson,
interview with Ian Thom,
November 1992

they share with art made for the Haida themselves certain aesthetic characteristics. But, as commodities produced for circulation outside the community, they are "tainted" by commercialism and a measure of inauthenticity. Works specifically commissioned for museums become, almost ironically, "genuine" images of an extinct, unchanging tradition. The post-Edenshaw works of twentieth-century carvers, languishing in their crudeness, become clear manifestations of the loss inherent in the final fall. Then, the story goes, redemption occurred by means of the Northwest Coast renaissance, when excellence and virtuosity would once again dominate the creation of art.[86] Parallelling this almost biblical narrative is the movement from purity to contamination and back, finally, to purity.

Troubling in this account is the implicit stifling of voices of those who thought it acceptable and appropriate to make art for sale, regardless of its adherence to a canon. While the reappearance of the canon is a positive feature of Haida art, it does not follow that noncanonical art deserves dismissal. In this age when many voices, especially those of Native people themselves, speak and are listened to, we need not—indeed must not—be exclusionary. Similarly, we must recognize that room exists for many expressions of Haida artistic traditions: those which are fine, and those which are not; those which remain within the community, and those which go outside; those which adhere to long-standing formal and symbolic conventions, and those which radically depart from them. I intentionally take a nonevaluative perspective here to avoid adding further despairing notes to this narrative.

The challenge of Northwest Coast art history is to incorporate into its discourse contributions to rather than negations of the ongoing postcolonial efforts at liberation by acknowledging history and recognizing expressions of endurance. We might gain some insights in this by considering an anecdote Robert Davidson tells about a song which contains the word *7eeyaa*, which translates to "I'm in awe." He wanted to create a mask for this song, but was unsure how to convey its message. So he consulted his grandmother, asking how to make a mask that puts you in awe; she responded, "You're allowed to create new masks and give them expression—just make this one smile." The answer ignored the application of formal canons. Instead, it penetrated to a level of creativity that accepts and even celebrates the complex history of Haida art. As Davidson puts it: "That made me realize that the masks aren't rigid, that there's a great deal of leeway permitted in the creation of masks. This was one of my most important breakthroughs, which I needed to go beyond the constraints imposed on my creativity. I needed this to go beyond an anthropological understanding of my culture."[87]

Robert Davidson's inventive ceremonialism, his drive to more deeply understand his traditions and his language, his sensitivity to his patrons, his willingness to participate as an artist in his community as well as in the international arena, and his continual search for the "soul" he saw in the art of his Haida elders all contribute to his compelling and numerous masterpieces. The optimistic smile of a mask, complementing a strength that inspires a profound and irresistible awe, can stand as a symbol of this contemporary master. Davidson embraces a multifaceted tradition of artists—anonymous as well as named, past, present and future—who powerfully disprove the myth of their disappearance.

I am proud to be one of those people chosen to put the pieces of the puzzle back together and move on. We have been stagnant now for three generations, and the challenge is ours to keep expanding the circle.
—Robert Davidson, 20 October 1991, New York

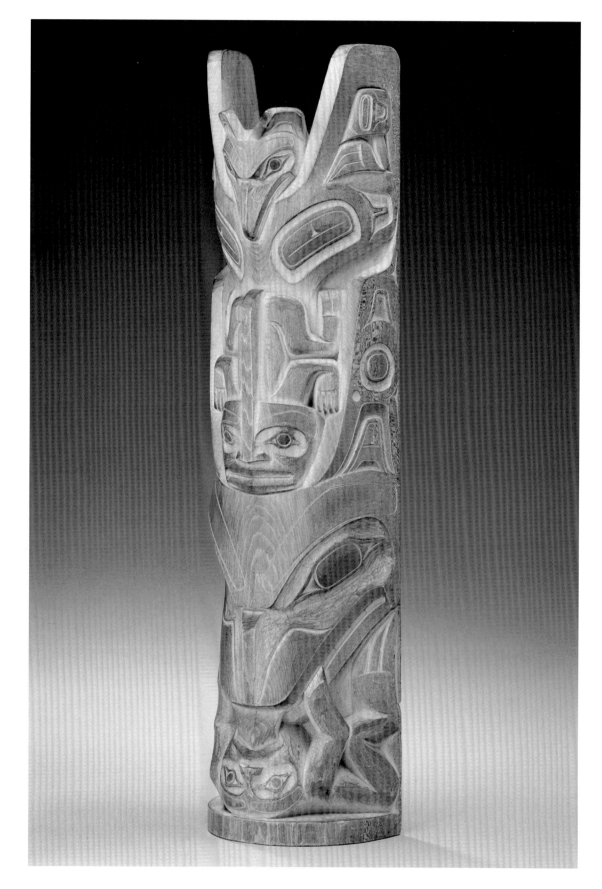

Raven Model Pole 1977

Yellow cedar

33.2 x 8.7 x 5.7 cm

SELECTED WORKS

1960–1979

Frog 1968

Screenprint: black on

cream heavy wove paper

Folded greeting card,

total sheet 16.2 x 24.9 cm

R. Davidson

Dogfish 1969

Screenprint: red on black

heavy wove paper

45.7 x 50.8 cm

Sea Bear Box Front 1969

Screenprint: black, red

on beige paper

66.3 x 51.2 cm

Sea Bear Box Back 1969

Screenprint: red, black

on beige paper

64.7 x 49.6 cm

31

Dogfish 1969

Screenprint: red, black

on beige wove paper

Folded greeting card,

total sheet 9.5 x 44.4. cm

PRIVATE COLLECTION

FACING PAGE:

Sugar Bowl 1968

Alder

5.8 x 9.3 x 7.5 cm

PRIVATE COLLECTION

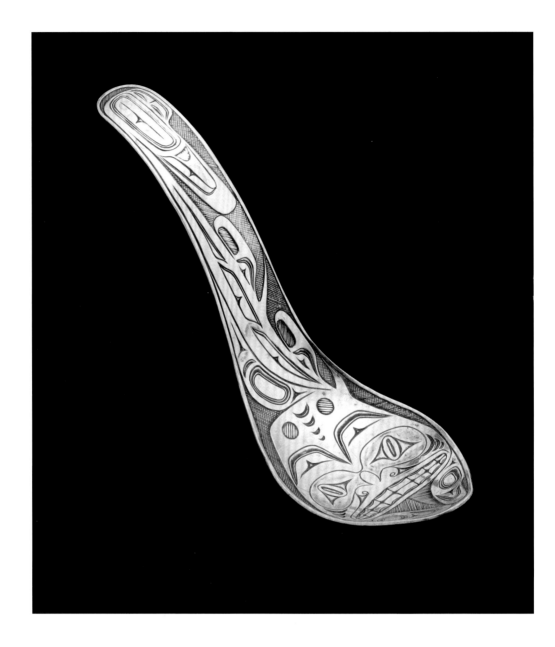

Dogfish Spoon 1970

Silver

11.5 x 3.8 x 9

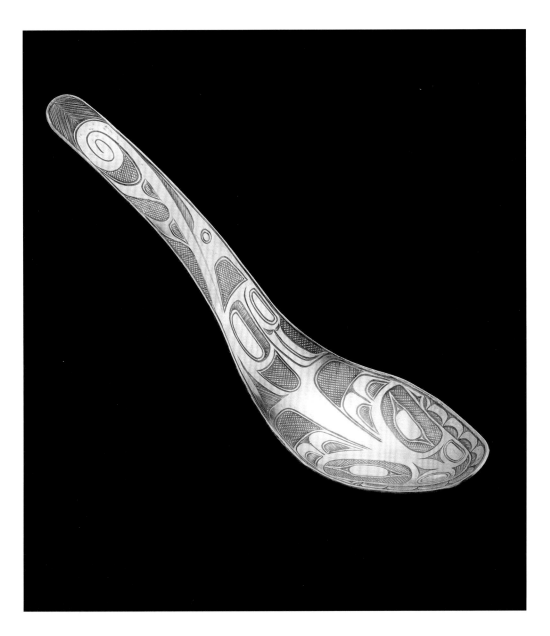

Dogfish Spoon 1971

Silver

11 x 3 x 4.5 cm

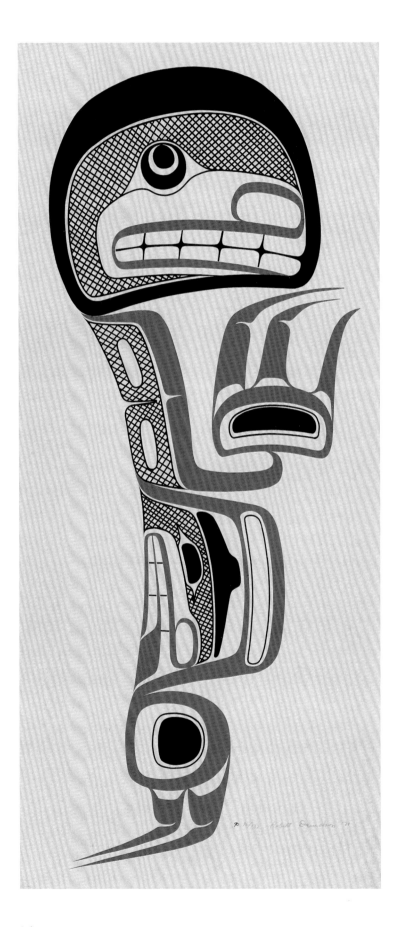

Human 1971

Screenprint: black, red on

brown paper

63.5 x 28.5 cm

PRIVATE COLLECTION

36

Dogfish 1971
Screenprint: black, red
on cream Arches paper
76.2 x 33.2 cm

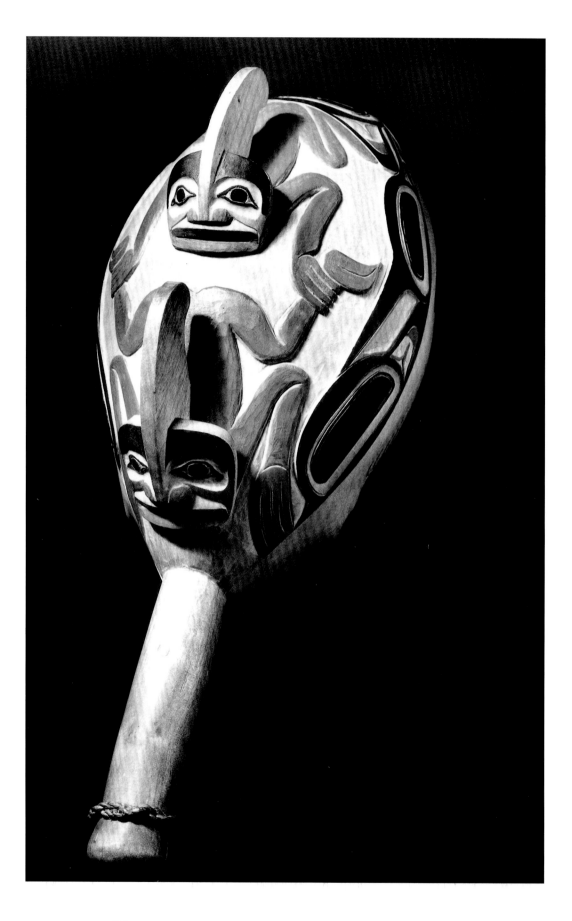

Dogfish Rattle 1971
Back and front views
Alder, cedar bark, acrylic
28.8 x 12 x 15.3 cm
ROYAL BRITISH
COLUMBIA MUSEUM,
13901

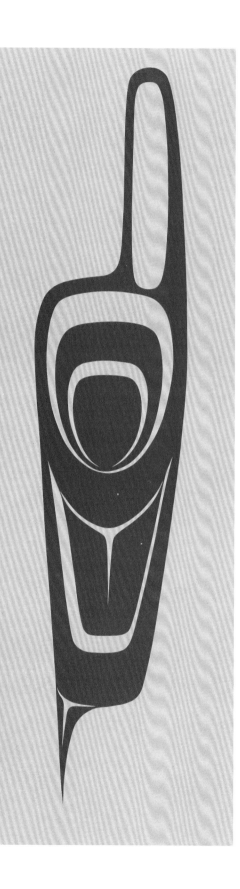

LEFT:

Feather Designs 1972

Screenprint: red on beige

wove paper

53.3 x 17.8 cm

PRIVATE COLLECTION

RIGHT:

Feather Designs 1972

Screenprint: red on black

wove paper

53.3 x 17.8 cm

PRIVATE COLLECTION

Raven Stealing the Moon
1977
Screenprint: black, red
on beige Arches paper
76.6 x 43.2 cm
PRIVATE COLLECTION

Raven Stealing the Moon
Panel 1972
Red cedar
213 x 90.6 x 3.9 cm
PRIVATE COLLECTION

Wolf
Bracelet 1972
Silver
2.6 x 6.1 x 5.1
PRIVATE COLLECTION

Bracelet 1972
Silver: 6.5 cm diameter,
3.8 cm height
MUSEUM OF ANTHRO-
POLOGY, UNIVERSITY OF
BRITISH COLUMBIA,
A17116

FACING PAGE:
Frog 1974
Screenprint: red, black on
brown heavy wove paper
32.4 x 28.6 cm
PRIVATE COLLECTION

RD 74   Robert Davidson   1974

Human Maskette 1974

Alder, paint

11.5 x 10.4 x 6.5 cm

PRIVATE COLLECTION

Eagle Mask 1973

Red cedar, oil-based paint

106 x 77 x 37 cm

PRIVATE COLLECTION

Salmon Bracelet 1974

Silver

4.5 x 6.5 x 5.7 cm

PRIVATE COLLECTION

FACING PAGE:

Raven with Broken Beak

1974

Screenprint: red on beige

wove paper

14 x 18 cm

PRIVATE COLLECTION

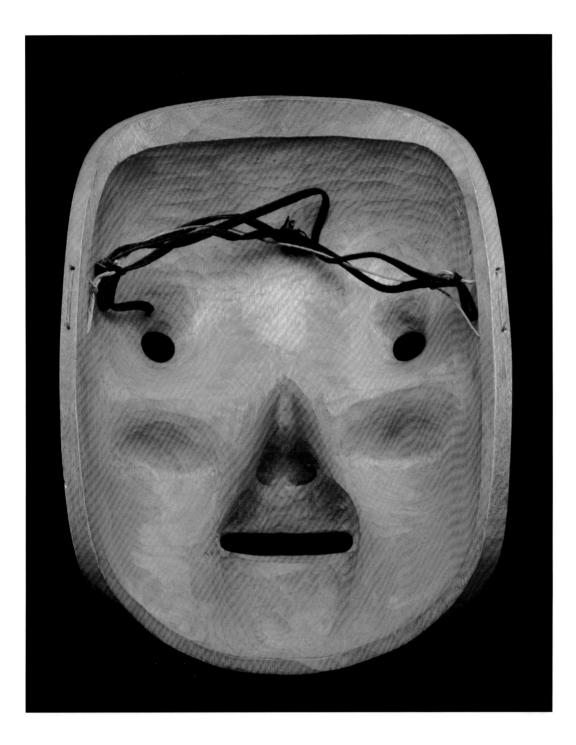

Woman with Labret

Mask 1975

Front and back views

Alder, paint

20.5 x 15.5 cm

PRIVATE COLLECTION

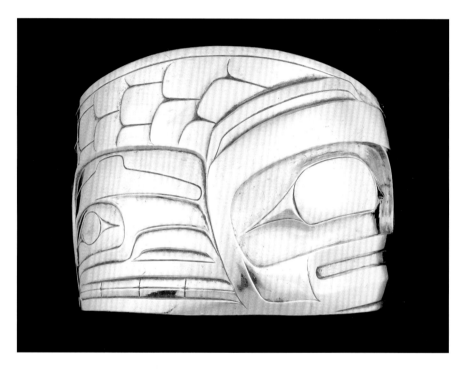

Raven Bracelet 1975
Silver
5.2 x 6.7 x 5.7 cm
PRIVATE COLLECTION

Beaver Bracelet 1975
Silver
3.8 x 6 x 5.5 cm
PRIVATE COLLECTION

Raven with Broken Beak

1975

Screenprint: red, black

on cream wove paper

35 x 28 cm

Negative and Positive

1975

Screenprint: red, black
on beige wove paper
Folded greeting card,
total sheet 44.4 x 9.5 cm

Moon 1976
Screenprint: red, blue on
black heavy wove paper
43.3 x 43.5 cm
PRIVATE COLLECTION

Sea Monster 1976
Screenprint: blue, red on
heavy beige wove paper
36.8 x 36.9 cm
PRIVATE COLLECTION

Butterfly Pendant 1976

Silver

3.6 x 2.9 x 0.3 cm

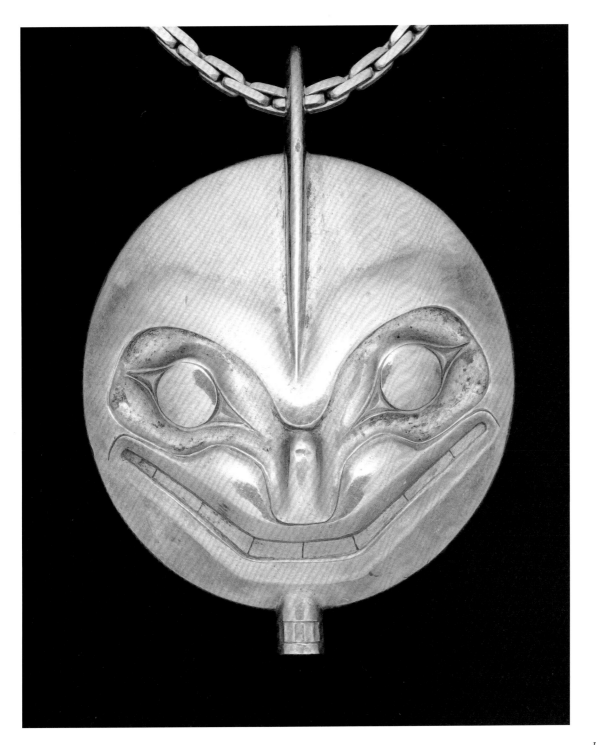

Killer Whale Rattle
Pendant 1976
Silver (goat horn handle
missing)
7.7 x 5.7 x 1.5 cm
PRIVATE COLLECTION

55

Frog Mask 1976

Alder

17.3 x 17.6 x 11.5 cm

Frontlet 1977
Pearwood, acrylic,
abalone
17.7 x 15.3 x 8 cm

FACING PAGE:
Eagle 1979
Screenprint: red, black
on beige Arches paper
53.4 x 53.4 cm

Four Circles: Raven with Broken Beak 1977
Screenprint: red, black
on cream wove paper
20.4 x 20.4 cm

Four Circles: Eagle 1977
Screenprint: red, black
on cream wove paper
20.4 x 20.4 cm

Four Circles: Killer Whale
1977
Screenprint: black, red
on cream wove paper
20.4 x 20.4 cm
PRIVATE COLLECTION

Four Circles: Frog 1977
Screenprint: black, red
on cream wove paper
20.4 x 20.4 cm
PRIVATE COLLECTION

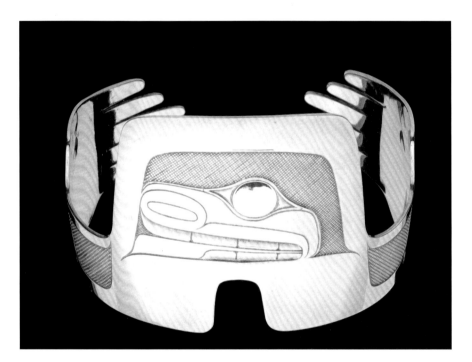

Hugging the World
Bracelet 1979
Silver
4.4 x 6.2 x 4.8 cm
PRIVATE COLLECTION

FACING PAGE:
Eagle Model Pole 1977
Yellow cedar
33.1 x 8.6 x 5.5 cm
PRIVATE COLLECTION

Model Pole 1959

Yellow cedar

27.2 x 4.7 x 4.3 cm

THE EVOLUTION
OF AN ARTIST

by Ian M. Thom

Whatever directions he pursues, he will not forfeit the richness of content or unrelenting perfectionism which are his mark.[1]

At a party to celebrate a collector's acquisition of a work by his wife, Dorothy Grant, Robert Davidson sees a drum hanging on the wall. Taking down the drum, Davidson tells the group that he will sing the first Indian song he knew. He beats the drum and begins to sing: "One little, two little, three little Indians . . ."

A story that Davidson tells is that when he was a child he enjoyed watching movies and television shows about cowboys and Indians. He cheered for the cowboys, until one day his uncle took him aside and told him he was an Indian. Davidson cried because the Indians were always the bad people, and he did not want to be one of the bad people.

These stories reveal much about Davidson and his journey as both an artist and a man. His art and his life have been largely about defining who he is and what it means to be Haida and, more particularly, what it means to be Haida within the context of a white world. The story of his art is firstly the story of a remarkable recovery of the Haida artistic vocabulary and, subsequently, a growth in consciousness and awareness which has led to an expansion of that vocabulary. It is the story of an art awakening and growing by gradual measures. Davidson, who is now in mid-career, can look back at an evolution of over thirty years even though he is only in his forties.

Davidson began his career influenced by his grandfather Robert Davidson Sr. and father, Claude.[2] It was because his father "insisted that he start carving"[3] that Davidson produced his first model pole *(page 64)*. Claude Davidson himself had started to do some carving and Robert Davidson Sr. had always been a boatbuilder and later a carver. There had not, however,

My grandfather would tell me stories about the totem pole, and different rituals that I had to do. One of them was with the totem pole—before it could be raised—I had to carry all the tools that I used. I tied them all together and carried them around my neck, over my shoulders and chant, chant this call. It was really a powerful feeling I had when it happened. It happens in just about any medium, when you have this real high.

—Robert Davidson, interview with Carol Sheehan McLaren, Canadian Conservation Institute, August 1978, Massett, Haida Gwaii

65

been a strong tradition of carving in young Robert's childhood village of Old Massett, and therefore this small pole, crudely carved though it is, is important as a first artistic statement. A copy of a pole by Robert Davidson Sr.,[4] it is a simple compilation of crest images: Eagle (one of the two principal Haida crests and Davidson's own crest), Frog (which, interestingly, has become for Davidson his "helper spirit"), Raven (the other major Haida crest) and Bear.

In spite of its simplicity, the pole reveals some of the traits present in all of Davidson's later work—an exceptional economy and an ability to utilize the shorthand of Haida form, here seen in the compact Raven, which is largely beak, eye and upturned tail. Apart from this early experience with wood, Davidson's career begins with argillite, the carbonaceous shale which is quarried only in Haida Gwaii (the Queen Charlotte Islands). Just thirteen when he carved his first argillite model pole,[5] Davidson gained knowledge quickly; he would carve a pole and show it to either his father or grandfather, who would correct the work. Soon Davidson was earning money from selling his argillite poles and continued to do so after his move to Vancouver to complete high school in 1965.

Argillite originally came into use as a material for tourist art. Argillite objects were first made for sale to visiting traders, but the stone became a major medium of expression for several distinguished Haida artists, most notably Davidson's great-grandfather Charles Edenshaw. Davidson began by copying, and, as Hilary Stewart has noted, early poles show the influence of his grandfather.[6] It was some time before Davidson was able to fully grasp the complexity of the mature style of Edenshaw.

Argillite allowed Davidson to express himself, but perhaps the most significant consequence of his use of this medium was his introduction to the distinguished Haida carver Bill Reid.[7] His time with Reid was short, but it allowed Davidson to consider the role of the artist and to hone his skills. He began to think graphically: he worked on flat images for the first time and was introduced to silver and the art of engraving.

Davidson had drawn as a child but had never transferred his interest in drawing to Haida motifs. His drawing was generally copying. He did not perceive of drawing as either a compositional tool or an end in itself. Initially, with Reid's guidance, he continued to copy, but now he drew on copper plates *(page 68)*. These practice plaques are tightly drawn and lack the flow of line which Davidson was soon to achieve. Early bracelets, such as the *Raven* bracelet, are substantially freer in form and reveal the alacrity with which Davidson achieved command of the material.

Davidson's work with Reid was largely in silver, but the two also carved a wooden totem pole together. In the Native tradition of showing rather than telling, Reid carved one side and Davidson the other. This work was of critical importance to Davidson because it demonstrated his skill and expertise to the older artist. Reid's confidence in Davidson led him to recommend Davidson as a carving teacher for the school in 'Ksan. The Gitanmaax School of Northwest Coast Indian Art at 'Ksan (near Hazelton in northern British Columbia) was established in the mid-1960s to teach Native art traditions.

In 1967, Davidson left his studies with Reid and enrolled in the Vancouver School of Art.[8] In retrospect, Davidson regards the time at art school as being important for its emphasis on drawing. During this period he began to draw extensively, both as a testing ground for ideas and to define the final form of a project. His notebooks served as a repository for the quick, intuitive drawings which continue to be the first expression of his ideas. Davidson's formal studies in design were fairly basic, but they forced him to confront the process of his art; what had been largely intuitive became more focussed.

His other significant activity was the study of traditional Haida art. The present wealth of artistic activity in Haida Gwaii makes it difficult to realize that there was little to be seen during Davidson's childhood and early teenage years. Not only were artists not producing work but there were no collections of earlier art or utilitarian objects for Davidson to refer to. When Davidson visited the Vancouver Museum for the first time in 1966, the work he saw there was a revelation. He became a regular visitor and began to study the forms and the techniques of earlier artists, particularly Charles Edenshaw. In addition to this practical study, Davidson talked with Bill Reid and Doug Cranmer, and with scholars Bill Holm and Wilson Duff.

The period of time that Davidson spent in 'Ksan during 1968 was valuable in furthering his knowledge of indigenous artforms. Through teaching the forms of Tsimshian art and carving in that tradition, he became more acutely aware of the forms of Haida art. Although Davidson carved

There are only a very few people who are actually bringing the art back to its original form where it was an expression of the time. I feel more people have to do homework. I guess I'm echoing Bill Reid's sentiments. I'm not trying to put myself on a pedestal, but I feel that we all have to go through that training period before we can actually start innovating. I feel that sometimes the intent is missed. I feel that sometimes we get caught up in sales, so that sometimes governs the direction the art is going in. And so I feel that, for myself, I cannot replace the art from the language. I can't replace the fact that Haida art is now becoming written. It doesn't change my attitude towards the art as an expression.
—Robert Davidson, interview with Ian Thom, November 1992

Wolf Plaque 1969–70

Copper

5 x 4 cm

Marriage Announcement

1969

Screenprint: black on

cream heavy wove paper

14 x 18 cm

two poles in the Tsimshian style while in 'Ksan, he did few carvings in Haida style. A notable work from the period is a Haida-style *Frog (page 124)*, which was originally carved as a trophy. Although broadly handled, the image has an energy and a life-force which ideally match the subject. The carving has a vitality which suggests that found in a frog itself. The stylized forms of a frog's attributes—wide mouth, bulbous eyes, large webbed feet—complement the more naturalistic, swelling forms of the carving itself. It is a frog which might well leap away.

The second event associated with Davidson's sojourn in 'Ksan was the production of his first screenprint *(page 27)*. As Stewart has noted, Davidson had been introduced to the basics of screenprinting in high school.[9] Using this knowledge, he decided to print an invitation to a showing of the work of his students at 'Ksan.[10] Davidson chose a Frog and copied the design from a dance blanket in the nearby Hazelton Museum; while naturally lacking the plasticity of the carved frog, the image also lacks the movement found in his carving and jewelry of the period. The artist chose to print the image using black or red ink, and placed the image on a cream or brown background. These backgrounds suggest the brown of wood and relate to the history of painted boxes and drums with which Davidson was now somewhat familiar. The tension resulting from the fact that the image is neither a painted box nor drum is, however, manifest in the flatness of the design, which sits uneasily on the page. The print was, nevertheless, admirably suited to its purpose and marked the beginning of Davidson's printmaking. Pleased with the first print, he did another later that fall, again using a dance blanket as a source.

The following year, 1969, Davidson was again studying in Vancouver and made a number of experimental, non-Haida pieces of jewelry in his classes. He practised techniques of repoussé and relief carving and sought advice on his screenprinting. Early that year, Davidson married Susan Thomas, whom he had met in 'Ksan. To mark the occasion, Davidson produced a startlingly original screenprint *(page 69)*[11] which shows his growing maturity as a designer. The suppleness of the line and the balance of the blacks to "whites" are accomplished and recall the energy of the *Frog* carving. Davidson, a member of the Eagle clan, is represented at the left, while his first wife, who is not a Native and had not yet been adopted into a Haida family, is on the right. Clearly a human figure, she is given long hair, depicted in strokes which suggest the incising found on argillite figures. She is also endowed with human hands, but her feet are the claws of a bird (an oblique reference to the fact that Davidson as an Eagle must marry a Raven). A further subtlety introduced into this work is something rarely seen in Northwest Coast prints: the overlapping of the hand of Susan Davidson and the arm/wing of Robert Davidson. The idea of union is simply and elegantly expressed.

The major project of 1969 was, however, the carving of a pole for Massett, the village of Davidson's childhood. He has often commented on the importance of this pole and its significance for him, but it is doubtful that he was aware then of the full import of his actions. Only twenty-three, Davidson was to carve the first pole in nearly fifty years, and the events associated with the raising of the pole proved to be something of a watershed in reintroducing ceremony into the lives of the Haida. The artist deliberately chose three Grizzly Bears and three Watchmen, crests which did not belong exclusively to either Eagle or Raven clans, in order to make it clear that the pole was for all of the people.[12] He was assisted in the project by his brother Reg Davidson, and as the pole came to completion, he received extensive advice from his grandparents as to the form of the celebratory potlatch.

Although Davidson's was by no means the first of the modern potlatches, it was of great significance. He began to address issues of Haida ceremony in the design of button blankets and in the carving of a mask for the ceremony.[13] Although the mask was not completed in time for the potlatch and has now disappeared, it is interesting to note that the first of Davidson's masks was begun with the intention of being danced.

Upon his return to Vancouver after the raising of the pole, Davidson resumed his studies of screenprinting, jewelry and argillite carving. The confidence displayed in a carving such as the *Bear, Raven and Eagle* model pole *(page 18)* is remarkable when compared with his previous work, particularly the early wooden model pole.

Davidson was the first Haida artist to exploit the screenprint in a significant way,[14] and the years 1969–70 saw the production of some fourteen prints. He also began to produce prints in two colours and developed the habit of preparing a full-scale cartoon drawing of each image.

Davidson regards all his work as "experimental" and feels strongly that

When Robert raised the pole in 1969, there had been a real hunger for it. Even now, I believe, the younger artists have something to look at and identify with.
—Chief Alex Jones, interview with Ian Thom, July 1992

As it turned out, the totem pole became the medium for transferring knowledge. It became an occasion to celebrate one more time for my grandparents' generation. It became the school for cultural knowledge to be expressed, knowledge that could not be interviewed out of them. It gave reason for them to celebrate. It rekindled the spark. It sparked memories for ceremony, it joined art with ceremony. It sparked memories for songs to be sung again. I was not brought up hearing songs, or their beliefs. The people shone one more time.
—Robert Davidson, 20 October 1991, New York

it is crucial for any Haida artist to have a command of the vocabulary of the art. His own command of the vocabulary and his increasing ability to deal with the flat reality of a print is evidenced in the pair of prints *Sea Bear Box Front* and *Sea Bear Box Back (pages 30 and 31)*. A composite image,[15] the drawing of the image for the box back is an exercise in design. Davidson drew elements from a number of sources, and, although the upper corners of the image seem constrained, the balance in the main face is carefully controlled, and the ebb and flow of the line are elegant and telling. It is startling to realize that the *Frog* print *(page 27)*, which has no such sense of flow, was done only a year earlier. What is also striking is the clarity with which the image is articulated. The use of the two colours—red and black—brings the image into a focus which is not initially apparent in the drawing.

Davidson was busy on several fronts and in 1970 was asked to demonstrate carving for the summer in Montreal at Man and His World. Man and His World was the continuation of Expo '67 which, in 1970, highlighted Canada's indigenous peoples. The resulting 3-m (10-foot) pole was given to the City of Montreal. Later that same year, Davidson travelled to Dublin as Canada's representative at the World Council of Craftsmen conference. His pole was presented as a gift to the Republic of Ireland, which in turn ceded it to the City of Dublin.[16] The Dublin pole is classic Haida in style: a Raven with two subsidiary figures, a Frog and a human face. The carving is in relatively shallow relief, but there is an accomplished balance between flat and carved areas, and those areas which are painted and not.

The Dogfish or Shark motif appears extensively in Davidson's work, and the examination of a spoon from 1970 *(page 34)* and two prints from 1969 and 1971 *(pages 29 and 37)* which use that motif demonstrates his changing approach to design. Although *Dogfish (page 32)* is initially a complex image, with a lively variety of line and the inclusion of both human and animal faces in the fins, it is bisymmetrical and holds relatively close to the norms of Haida composition. Each row of spines is matched to the other, and the curved tail is split. The head of the Dogfish has three sets of gills, something which Davidson often includes in his work.

The spoon introduces something new. As Joan Lowndes points out,

Davidson got bored with repeating the same design on both sides of his silver bracelets. He decided sometimes to tilt his central motif, thereby setting up a different form flow. The gracefully slanted lines created new divisions of the field, which in turn gave greater scope in the manipulation of design elements. This development grew out of the artist's engraved silver spoons. The decoration on their bowls is symmetrical, representing the head of an animal, bird or fish, whereas into the handle are fitted Northwest Coast style units, freely arranged in a refined, asymmetrical pattern.[17]

The forgoing might easily serve as a description of this spoon. Davidson has retained much of the head of the previous Dogfish, notably the fleur-de-lys nose and three sets of gills, but the graceful tail fitted into the handle is quite another story. The spiky back bends gracefully around to be accommodated in the handle. This change serves two functions. First, it introduces a sense of movement into what had, in the print, been a static subject, but more importantly it allows for the complex play of differing patterns of line. Davidson uses parallel hatching, cross-hatching and chevron shapes in addition to the more straightforward line of engraving. This variety serves to direct the eye and animate the whole.

Asymmetry is used to a marked degree in two prints from early in 1971, *Human (page 36)* and *Raven with a Broken Beak and the Blind Halibut Fisherman*, as well as the sinuous *Dogfish (page 37)*. The lessons learned in the spoon are splendidly realized here. As with the spoon, the image is "weighted at the base, curving up and over into a long S shape."[18] The effect is one of movement and force, accentuated by the strong pattern of the black formline. The secondary red plays only an accent role and as such enhances the strong drawing of the main body of the fish.

Davidson was becoming more confident of his abilities with the silkscreen medium, and despite the fact that he had yet to receive much commercial success, he continued to push the bounds of his experience. His willingness to change and adapt Haida iconography to the needs of contemporary life—the 1971 change of address card is a good example—is indicative of what had become a driving force within his work: the desire to build upon and expand the vocabulary, not merely echo previous artists.

I'm creating the line, each line has its own tension. It's like bending a ruler—you're creating that tension. And my feeling about that tension is—you stop that tension before it breaks.
—Robert Davidson, interview with Dan Nadaner and Rob Wood, summer 1982

It becomes more and more challenging because you know that the circle is becoming very challenging, in coming up with new concepts. One of my biggest fears is that I'll become boring, so I'm always wanting to approach the circle with new ideas or fresh ideas so that the viewer is brought into the image.
—Robert Davidson, interview with Ian Thom, November 1992

Robert and Reg Davidson, Whonnock, 1974.

Sara's Birth Announcement

1973

Screenprint: black, red on

brown paper card

Folded greeting card, total

sheet 36.3 x 14.3 cm

The series of *Feather Designs (page 40)* are, as Stewart has pointed out, a study in technique.[19] Davidson was anxious to "test his skill in cutting and pulling prints."[20] The design itself is very simple, but the balance of voids and solids, positives and negatives, is both elegant and controlled. The line is carefully modulated, and he has made excellent use of the shaped sheet of paper. The preparatory drawings reveal that the process of creating a line which bends but does not break was a time-consuming one; the contours were subtly adjusted to introduce tension but not break.

In 1971, Davidson moved to Whonnock (near Vancouver) in order to secure a studio large enough to work on full-size totem poles. His domestic life in Whonnock was a satisfying one, and 1973 marked the birth of his first child, Sara. Davidson's wife, Susan, had been adopted into the Raven clan in 1969 and thus could be depicted as a Raven in the iconography of crests. This important personal event, like his marriage, called for a card to mark the occasion. He produced two designs and asked his wife to choose between them. *Raven and Fetus* "depicted his wife as a Raven, portraying her in a protective attitude, head and beak bent down, sheltering the small unborn Raven that has its wings and legs bent in the upside-down pre-birth position."[21] The artist has made two subtle distinctions in this elegant design. First is the depiction of the unborn child as both Raven and human (the fetus is clearly marked as human by the peaked eyebrow formline). Second is the use of three distinct eye shapes, which define a variety of solutions to the problem of the eye socket and pupil. This seemingly minor point is indicative of Davidson's strong intuitive design sense and his desire to push himself.

It was, however, the first of Davidson's two designs *(page 74)* that was used as the announcement,[22] and it is perhaps "the most astonishing image he has ever created, combining crest heraldry with realism."[23] The immediacy and power of the birth process is clearly seen in the gesture of the Raven/mother grasping her knees as she bears down to bring the child into the world. The depiction of lungs and the birth canal, the suggestion that the baby is pushing herself into the world, and the powerful linear pattern, all combine to give this image a particular resonance. Davidson made an interesting choice in depicting his wife as a Raven with a broken beak: this allowed him to more clearly depict her as both Raven and human and echo the head shape of the emerging child.

Much of Davidson's most inventive work of his early career was created, as Lowndes has noted, to mark personal occasions.[24] This is also true of his jewelry: the 1973 *Butterfly* bracelet *(page 76)* is an exceptional work within the Haida canon. The exterior of the bracelet is plain except for the Kugganjad (Mouse Woman)—but on the inside is an extraordinary, elongated Butterfly (recognizable by its long proboscis). The variety of handling and detail is dazzling. Within a limited vocabulary of line, Davidson has varied shapes and forms, placing ovoids slightly acentrally, using the egg-shaped oval of which he is so fond to introduce rhythm and flow into the composition. The piece has an audacity and strength that suggest Davidson was a fully mature artist, despite the fact he was still in his twenties.

In fact, in the 1970s, Davidson produced a number of highly important pieces of jewelry (principally bracelets), the designs for which he would often translate into other media. These bracelets were an arena for considerable change within his work. As Alan Hoover has pointed out, as early as 1970 Davidson had introduced asymmetry into his bracelets,[25] stretching a figure around the circumference with head at one end and tail at the other. This represented a considerable advance on the "standard classic Edenshaw split format."[26] In the *Tcamous* (*Snag* or *Living Log*) bracelet *(page 76)* of 1975, Davidson used "out-size design elements"[27] and thus clarified the design.

As Hoover suggests, this eventually led Davidson back to the design principles of Edenshaw,[28] but symmetry was explored in a new way. In the *Whale* bracelet *(page 77)* of 1979, the two Whales are presented in an unexpected form; without lower jaws, the images are completed "by maintaining the shape of the missing jaws as negative space."[29] The final twist is that the heads are "each a mirror image of the other."[30]

It is worth noting that this independence of spirit anticipates that seen in most of his later bracelets, such as *Happy Negative Spaces* of 1980 *(page 77)*. This direction in Davidson's work represents what Hoover suggests is complete mastery of Haida design grammar. It is because Davidson's mastery is complete that he is able to innovate within that vocabulary and thus expand the possibilities of Haida design.

The advance in Davidson's command of the bracelet form was accompanied by similar shifts and movement within his screenprints and carv-

West Coast art is very disciplined and very precise, very stylized, but it also has a lot of room for innovation and creativity.
—Robert Davidson, interview with Ian Thom, November 1992

I always felt that the positive space was the important thing, but as I developed as an artist and as a person, I started realizing how important those negative spaces were. Whenever you create a space, you create another space.
—Robert Davidson, interview with Dan Nadaner and Rob Wood, summer 1982

75

Butterfly Bracelet 1973
Silver
1.7 x 6.2 x 5.5 cm
PRIVATE COLLECTION

Tcamous (Living Log)
Bracelet 1975
Silver
3.9 x 5.4 x 6.2 cm
ROYAL BRITISH
COLUMBIA MUSEUM,
cat. 18827

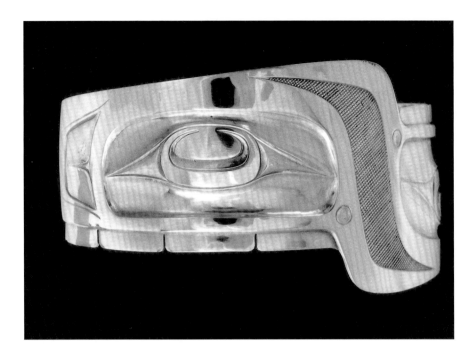

Whale Bracelet, 1979
Silver
3.7 x 5.3 x 6.8 cm
ROYAL BRITISH
COLUMBIA MUSEUM
cat. 16601

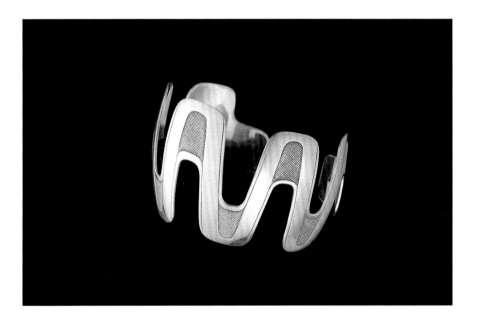

Happy Negative Spaces
Bracelet 1980
Silver
4.3 x 6.4 x 6 cm
ROYAL BRITISH
COLUMBIA MUSEUM,
cat. 18826

Then, I did a lot of argillite. I remember during my learning process of carving argillite I would go and visit all the carvers in the village here at Massett. Because anytime I want to do something or to learn it I put my whole heart into it and that's what I did. I just didn't go to one carver. I went to all of them. I saw all their workshops, their tools, their good ideas.

—Robert Davidson, interview with Carol Sheehan McLaren, Canadian Conservation Institute, August 1978, Massett, Haida Gwaii

ing. Much of Haida traditional art was applied to utilitarian objects, and Davidson is no exception in this regard; he has produced a number of wooden bowls and utensils. A simple sugar bowl of 1976 *(page 33)* displays his ability to use and adapt Haida design within a wood tradition. Just as an earlier silver box had adapted the design conventions of the painted bent-box, Davidson's adaptation of his skills as a flat designer are seen in his bowls. The identity of the design with the surface is remarkable; the design swells as the form of the object swells. In the 1970s, Davidson explored a variety of woods—alder, pear, red and yellow cedar, and was introduced to boxwood by Bill Reid.[31]

The results of his exploration can be seen in three objects from the early 1970s: the *Woman with Labret* mask *(pages 48 and 49)*, the *Human* maskette *(page 45)*, and the large *Eagle* mask *(page 44)*. The *Eagle* is a "mask" in the sense of being a single object which could be used in a ceremony, but it was never intended as such. It functions best in formal terms; an elegant flow of line traces the beak, and the pattern of the red and black paint serves to highlight the carved forms. The image has a stylized, somewhat iconic quality, which is accentuated by the simplification of the forms and the large scale.

The two human forms are, in contrast, more accessible. This is, of course, partly due to the subject matter, but not incidentally reflects the attention of the carver to the issues of both realism and design. The *Woman with Labret* mask is particularly striking in the suggestion that there is life within the wooden cheeks. The swelling forms, the high cheekbones and the finish all suggest this. The application of paint is restrained and serves to abstract the image. There is thus a tension between the impulse to read the object as portrait as opposed to type. The *Human* maskette displays a similar tension: the paint would suggest something outside our experience, but the carving itself evokes the smoothness of skin and the suggestion of bone beneath that skin. Davidson is a perfectionist, and this piece is notable for the sheer quality of the finish; the outside surface is silken and even the inside is finely carved. The next step, still several years away, was the creation of a mask for use in ceremony.

The year 1974 marked another change for Davidson: he gave up carving argillite.[32] He found that this material which he had been carving for more than ten years, was "just too dirty";[33] more importantly, he found the brittle medium uncongenial to his sense of form. One of the last argillite pieces he carved is a *Dogfish* platter *(page 81)*. It makes an instructive comparison to an alder mask of the same subject he carved in 1974 *(page 80)*. The platter design is asymmetrical, like the earlier spoon and print; there is a contrast between the stable head with the high forehead and the sweeping form of the body. Although the design reflects "the intellectual sharpness and controlled tension of the best of his precursors,"[34] it lacks the drama of three-dimensional carving and the movement of his bracelets.

The *Dogfish* mask has both movement and drama while maintaining the exacting carving techniques found in the argillite. The use of the block of alder is accomplished; there is a tension within the forms that suggests a spirit inhabiting the mask, and the balance of convex and concave forms, of linear pattern and carved areas, is delicate. Finally, the mask reflects Davidson's feeling for the wood, something seen in the *Woman with Labret* mask. The decision not to paint the mask, allowing sculpted form alone to make the statement, was a bold one. The fact that this mask was not intended for use and therefore did not have to function in a theatrical setting may have influenced his decision.

As Hilary Stewart has noted, Davidson frequently returns to ideas and themes, and by this process constantly refines them.[35] The shift between his 1974 small card *Raven with Broken Beak (page 47)* and the larger print of the same title in 1975 *(page 51)* is striking. Initially, it appears that Davidson has simply doubled the image and introduced the second colour (black) for the formlines. A closer examination reveals a series of shifts: refinements in the ovoids at the upper corners, an additional U-shape within the double eyes, greater definition in the human face below the beak, considerable elaboration within the wing of the Raven and an overall thinning of the formlines. The effect of these changes is a greater clarity and legibility. The claustrophobia that is felt in the earlier image is gone, and there is also a new sense of relief: the blacks inevitably move forward and the reds tend to recede.

The dialogue between black, white (or cream) and red which marks all of Davidson's early prints is at once restrained and rich. Although the artist was eventually to find this palette limiting, he used overprinting and

People always ask me what medium is my preference, but I always respond by saying my preference is the medium that I am excited about at that moment. If it is wood then I do a lot of wood, but if it is silkscreening I do a lot of prints. The only way I feel I can develop in a medium is to work on it for a few months. I just can't work on it sporadically.
—Robert Davidson, interview with Carol Sheehan McLaren, Canadian Conservation Institute, August 1978, Massett, Haida Gwaii

79

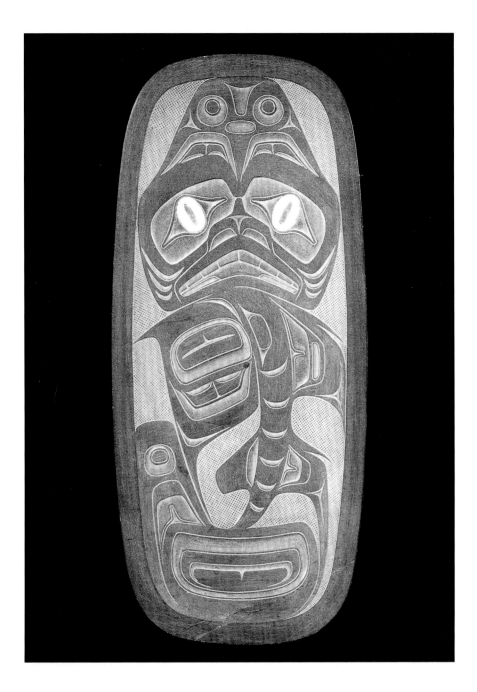

Dogfish Platter 1974
Argillite, abalone
3.6 x 14.1 x 3.8 cm
ROYAL BRITISH
COLUMBIA MUSEUM
cat. 14529

FACING PAGE:
Dogfish Mask 1974
Alder
14 x 29 x 20.6 cm
ROYAL BRITISH
COLUMBIA MUSEUM,
cat. 15119

*It is the ideas that are
brought into fruition that
are important. If they
work, then they become
part of the culture. If they
don't work, then they
become part of the
experience.*
—Robert Davidson,
20 October 1991,
New York

juxtapositions of these colours to telling effect. The red on black combination first seen in the 1972 *Feather Designs* is elaborated upon in the 1975 print *Negative and Positive (page 52)*. The use of the reversed and differently coloured heads and the "slits" top and bottom in the image gives the whole a strong sense of movement and transcends the modest scale of the image. The second notable aspect of this image is the use of a cross-hatched formline first seen in the *Human* print of 1971 *(page 36)*.

The following year, 1976, was an important one for Davidson; in addition to the birth of his son, Benjamin, it saw an important public commission, the *Reality and Interpretation (Sea Monster)* carved screen for the Canadian Broadcasting Corporation building in Vancouver. That year also marked the beginning of an important series of works using the circle.[36] Not a traditional Haida form and seldom used in older Haida art, the circle has become something of a signature for Davidson. An initial and "spirited"[37] exploration of the circle form within his prints is the 1976 series of *Moon* prints *(page 53)*. These "man in the moon" images include the crescent of the moon and a highly reduced human figure: eye, nostril, upper jaw, teeth and hand (the last with only three fingers).

The prints are also important because he introduces blue into his colour palette[38] and because he uses an unusual formline for the top of the head: parallel shading. He printed the design in a number of colour combinations: blue and black on cream paper, red and blue on black printed paper, and blue on black printed paper. The shifts in effect, between what functions as positive and what functions as negative space, are striking. Davidson deliberately plays with the colour, and the emotional impact of each of the images is quite distinct. The blue on black image has a nocturnal, otherworldly effect and seems to suggest the identity of the subject with the paper. It is flat. The red, blue and black image makes the human figure dominant; and in the blue and black combination, the moon and human figure are equal partners in the design. There is, in short, a complexity which is challenging both visually and intellectually. Finally, Hilary Stewart suggests that this image had a special meaning for Davidson: "He saw that the man in the moon was himself. The hand forming the mouth symbolized for him the use of his hands as a mouthpiece since he communicated through his art."[39]

This extended meditation on colour had immediate results. *Sea Mon-*

ster (page 53) and *Benjamin's Birth Announcement* both use the new blue colour extensively and both, significantly, avoid black altogether. The birth announcement is an image which relates directly to Davidson's personal experience; it is a portrait of his family and at the same time a highly considered design. Stewart describes the evolution of the image:

> As he left the hospital, elated by the spirituality of the event [the birth of his son], he came face to face with a half moon shining in a clear night sky. Davidson had been searching for an idea for the birth announcement card, and the moon once more took on a special meaning. . . . At the top is Benjamin with a newborn look: no teeth and an immature eye without the eyelid. Because he was born at the half moon, his father introduced a hidden subtlety by overprinting (blue on red) a vertical half moon within the baby's circle. . . . To the left is the mother, mature, with a labret in her lower lip; beneath is the artist, adult, with no lip ornament; and to the right is young Sara with a wide-eyed childish look and a labret to indicate that she is female.[40]

The image is indicative of Davidson's ongoing interest in exploring the subtleties of form. The changes in each of the circles are for a narrative purpose, but at the same time they function to enliven and animate the image. There is a sense of movement where one might not expect it. This circular motion is accentuated by the "slits" between circles.

The Sea Monster was the motif of a double-sided pendant Davidson had been commissioned to create in 1974. He used a circle form, with the creature bent around a central neutral space. The pendant is identical on either side, but the central void is treated differently, one finely and one heavily textured. The design is largely defined by fine linear patterns. When he transferred the Sea Monster to a screenprint in 1976, he broadened and simplified these patterns; he also "changed the whole feeling from density to lightness by scooping out the middle, then leaving similar plain areas around the ovoids and U-shapes."[41] The image is filled with energy and moves in "a counter-clockwise direction, conveying the movement of a writhing monster."[42] The image thus has a sense of narrative: the monster moves and potentially engulfs us at its centre.

This Sea Monster design was used again in his important carved screen *Reality and Interpretation*, which Joan Lowndes has described:

If we look at the knife edge in the form of a circle, let us look at what is on the inside of the circle as experience, culture, and knowledge, let us look at this as the past. If we look at the edge of the knife as the present moment, it is that thin line that we live on, it is that thin line that divides the past from the future. What is outside of the circle is yet to be experienced. In order to expand the circle, we must know what is inside the circle.
—Robert Davidson,
20 October 1991,
New York

Davidson working on a print, c. 1976.

*I feel more free in terms of
tradition. At one point I
was really rigid and stuck
within the confines of it.
But I find that in order for
me to retain my excite-
ment for it, I have to keep
creating new ideas and
directions.*
—Robert Davidson,
interview with
Dan Nadaner and
Rob Wood, summer 1982

But in the present circumstance he conceived of the circle as a lens, which depending on how it is focused can alter the appearance of the world. Hence he arrived at two circles side by side, one a reflection of the other. . . . It is only after considerable study that one can discern five subtle variants. They take the form of convex/concave juxtapositions and lines which, instead of being contained within a system, freely engage space. Are the latter, incised like delicate antennae, a metaphor for individual interpretation? It is part of a teasing strain in high Indian art to leave us with a conundrum as well as to suggest the deeper philosophical problem of defining "reality."[43]

The screen is, as Lowndes also points out, flawless in execution, Davidson is in absolute control of his tools and his medium. The panel is carved and engraved with a precision which matches exactly the ideas behind the work. While the image is a superb design, it is much more than that. Davidson has emerged as an artist and thinker, and this work challenges the mind even as it delights and satisfies the eye. The technical and artistic skills so evident in earlier carved panels such as *Raven Stealing the Moon* of 1972 *(page 41)*, are refined and strengthened.

The honing of skills seen in the earlier *Feather Designs (page 40)* is repeated, with greater attention to design, in the 1977 set of prints *Four Circles—Raven, Eagle, Killer Whale, Frog (pages 60 and 61)*, to which he would return later. In these prints, which are the first that Davidson had executed by another printer, the images are "unique in that each embodies only the essence of the creature it portrays through the minimal use of line. The negative and positive shapes interlock to provide the necessary identifying features with amazing economy of detail."[44]

The shifts in colour, balance and form which animate this series continue to be of interest to Davidson and can be seen in the *Butterfly* pendant *(page 54)* Davidson made for his daughter in 1976. By compressing the image into the circular format, he gives it movement and graphic drama, qualities repeated in the double print he made of the same subject.

The success of Davidson's graphic work is a result of his strong design sense and his willingness to expand the boundaries of the traditional art. As Lowndes and Hoover point out, Davidson has "gone beyond the traditional"[45] in his use of compressed ovoids, which may be stretched vertically or horizontally, and his shifting use of formlines. In a 1977 print such as *Wolf (page 87)*, the subject is almost subsumed, and as early as 1972, he created a bracelet which has as its subject ovoids and U-shapes. The "interchanging negatives and positives"[46] of a print such as *Wolf* (or no doubt the original bracelet) have a degree of complexity and movement which is Davidson's alone. Having "gone beyond the traditional" but not abandoned it, he now turned himself to a project which required him to reconsider the greatest of the traditional artists, Charles Edenshaw.

In 1977 Davidson was asked by Parks Canada to create a memorial to Charles Edenshaw in Massett. He suggested that he would provide a front wall for the longhouse that was being built by the government.[47] The housefront, done in Edenshaw's style, became the memorial. This was Davidson's most important work to date. Large in scale, it was also large in ambition. He would be competing with and in a sense surpassing Edenshaw himself. Davidson chose to begin the project by spending a great deal of time studying Edenshaw's works. Initially, he did not intend to copy an Edenshaw work but to absorb Edenshaw's vocabulary and work in his style. After examining a number of Edenshaw objects, Davidson decided to base his design on the back of a chief's seat. The Frog motif had to be altered to fit the shape of the housefront, and Davidson did so with a minimum of distortion of the Edenshaw original. The other fundamental difference was, of course, scale: the housefront would be massive, 10.7 m (35 feet) in width and 3.5 m (11 ½ feet) high at the peak.

This project not only dwarfed all previous ones, it also marked the first time in many years that the artist was to spend an extended time in his childhood village. Davidson was assisted by his brother Reg and another carver, Gerry Marks. The project, which required a special workshop being built, took almost all of 1977. Davidson had determined that, because the housefront faced the sea, it was important to carve the front in considerable relief so that it would survive the rigours of the weather and could be read from a distance. The painted decoration was kept to a minimum, reflecting the standards of Edenshaw's day. "As with a totem, Davidson carved the lead side, taking care to keep sufficiently ahead so that his two assistants had work to copy."[48] The housefront was a powerful and successful design. "Throughout there was a tantalizing dialogue between circles and ovoids as well as between positives and negatives in the black and unpainted circles distributed over the surface."[49]

Davidson on the beach at Old Massett, 1978.
PHOTO BY ULLI STELTZER

The longhouse was situated on the north side of the village, and I had two apprentices. All the time we were working on it, I stressed the importance of space, how one line relates to another line, or how the ovoid relates to the U-shape, or how the ovoid relates to the space around it. And I talked about the balance, and how fragile things were. We spent two years on the longhouse. The second year, we carved the four poles for inside.

—Robert Davidson, interview with Dan Nadaner and Rob Wood, summer 1982

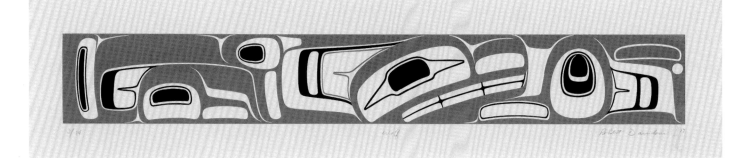

Wolf 1977
Screenprint: black, red
on cream wove paper
51 x 12 cm
VANCOUVER ART
GALLERY

FACING PAGE:
Dedication of the
Edenshaw memorial (left
to right): *Reg Davidson,*
Robert Davidson, Gerry
Marks at Old Massett,
1977.
PHOTO BY ULLI
STELTZER

A tribute to both Edenshaw and Davidson, the housefront, at least initially, inspired considerable enthusiasm. Davidson suggested to the Band Council that four house posts be carved for the interior.[50] This was done, under the auspices of a Canada Manpower project, with the assistance of eight apprentices (Reg Davidson and James Hart amongst them). Davidson had to plan a programme for the students to follow; they were to learn something about traditional Haida art (in a community where there was little of it) and how to make carving tools. They were taught to realize that "It's not mechanical. You've got to think."[51]

Since most of the work would be carried out by the students, Davidson produced maquettes for the house posts. These maquettes *(pages 24 and 63)* reflect the growth in his ability and originality since the earlier Massett pole of 1969. Representing Eagle and Raven, the maquettes display a command of the iconography of crests and a quality of carving which is striking. As Lowndes has commented, the motifs flow one into the other; the *Eagle* pole has "a face with a headdress that could simultaneously be read as the bird's tail feathers."[52] The *Raven* pole is similarly complex in design and points the way towards the form language of later images.

Davidson's new role in the community led him to reflect upon himself and his identity. An earlier print from 1976, *Transformation*, had suggested that people are complex. The image, a card with a pale red figure of a noblewoman, opens to reveal the same figure in a deeper shade of red. This suggests that the outer self "is only a pale image of the inner, deeper self; when that shallow outer cover opens, the real self beneath is revealed."[53]

A more elegant development of the idea is the 1979 print *Eagle (page 58)*. Here, Davidson has again used the circle, but it is a very elaborate one, with a black outer circle and red inner circle. The outer circle is the Eagle, the inner a Frog. Of this print Davidson has said: "The inner self, the heart, the gut reaction. Love. This is the first time I allowed the feeling to show, to help the outside. Without the inner frog, the eagle isn't complete. If you take the frog away, the eagle has no mouth."[54]

The inner and outer self are inextricably intertwined, something Davidson was coming to believe about Haida ceremony and what we call Haida art. This belief may be reflected in the self-portrait mask *After He Has Seen the Spirit . . . (page 90)*, which Davidson did after his major 1980 potlatch, "Tribute to the Living Haida."[55] This four-day celebration was very important for Davidson. It allowed him to assert his conviction that Haida art and culture should not dwell in the past. In order for living people to succeed, they had to move beyond the past, taking what was important and valuable but adapting these things to life now.

Regrettably, the Edenshaw house was not to last long. After being warmly welcomed by the community in 1978, it was burned down, probably by an arsonist, in August 1981. Perhaps because Davidson had become increasingly interested in ceremony and believed that all of Haida culture was part of a continuum, that art was not distinct from dancing or songs, he was able, after the initial shock, to conceive of a way to move beyond this experience. He had been planning a potlatch, "Children of the Good People," for November 1981. This celebration, his second potlatch, was to provide the forum for ending the mourning over the destroyed house.

The previous year, 1980, Davidson and Dorothy Grant had begun to design and execute ceremonial garments.[56] In keeping with his growing interest in Haida ceremony, he founded the Rainbow Creek Dancers and began to research, with the help of village elders in Massett, primarily his grandmother Florence Edenshaw Davidson, Haida dances and songs. He also had begun to produce drums for use in these ceremonies. These drums, which Davidson decorated as potlatch gifts in 1980, mark the beginning of his career as a painter.

Since the principal motif of the Edenshaw housefront was the Frog, he conceived the idea of a black *Frog* mask to symbolize the burnt house, and a dance to accompany the mask. Heavily burdened by preparations for the potlatch, Davidson asked his brother Reg to carve this mask. Late in the ceremonies accompanying the giving of names at the "Children of the Good People" potlatch, the mask was danced and afterwards burnt.[57] The dance and burning of the mask were cathartic for Davidson, and he immediately turned himself to other projects, the most notable being the exploration of painting.

It is hard for non-Haida people to understand that all of Davidson's prints prior to 1980 were based on black-and-white drawings, especially when the most effective of them rely so heavily on a sensitive use of colour. Painting, on drums and then on paper, freed him to work in a fluid

Cultural knowledge has been handed down through the generations by our elders. It was demonstrated through events such as name-giving feasts, totem-pole raisings, or potlatches. The potlatch is the supreme court where laws were made; ownership of songs, ownership of names, ownership of property demonstrated or challenged. Since the beginning, culture has made slow progress, each new succeeding generation acquiring the knowledge and giving meaning to that knowledge.
—Robert Davidson, comment at the publication of the book *Bill Reid*, April 1986, University of British Columbia Museum of Anthropology

After He Has Seen the Spirit . . . Mask 1980
Yellow cedar, acrylic,
operculum, leather,
feathers
16 x 42 x 21 cm
MUSEUM OF
ANTHROPOLOGY,
UNIVERSITY OF BRITISH
COLUMBIA (MOA SHOP
VOLUNTEERS FUND),
696/2

manner, and more importantly, allowed him to work graphically on an unprecedented scale.[58] The decision to paint on paper was critical. Although he had long used drawing as a laboratory to work out ideas, the translation to the final work inevitably meant a lessening of spontaneity. The actual task of cutting a screen or carving silver or wood was not conducive to the free flow of ideas. Painting, Davidson felt, allowed that; for although the artform itself has rules, there is a greater latitude for exploration when using a brush.

The first painting on paper, *Frog* in 1982, displays some lack of familiarity with the techniques and materials, and the gouache has not fared well. Perhaps because he was working in a new medium, Davidson made it symmetrical. What is unusual is the view; he splays out the head and provides an aerial view of the back, which he challengingly "depicts" as a void. Despite this, it is a rich image which relates back to the first *Frog* print of 1968 *(page 27)* and the print of 1974 *(page 43)*.

The group of large-scale works from 1983 *(pages 103, 104 and 105)* are both a more important statement and a challenge to the artist himself and Haida tradition. These highly abstracted images are larger than any of his others, and the resultant prints were so large that they initially met with resistance.[59] Although the scale was a problem for some collectors, it may have been the unorthodox use of the alphabet of Haida art—the ovoids and U-shapes (full and split)—which caused more consternation. Most of the images use cross-hatched formlines and one, *Every Year the Salmon Come Back (page 104)*, uses blue formlines!

One of the finest of this series of images is *T-Silii-AA-Lis, Raven Finned Killer Whale (page 103)*. The Raven has become humanoid, complete with a lower jaw which is the thumb, and the Whale itself is only suggested by the expanse of black upon which the image sits. The variety and flexibility of the artist's design is seen in the series of ovoids, all of which have differing shapes. Finally, the image is endowed with a sense of forward motion, right to left, by the series of irregular "slits" in the background black. The paintings and their related prints move Davidson's image-making into another realm; in the use of colour (the application of the paint often varies in the paintings), there is a vigour and visual boldness which is startling to those who are more familiar with traditional forms.

The major project for 1984 was a commission for three related poles to

Sometimes I'll doodle and it doesn't look right, and I'll doodle some more. Then maybe a day later, a week later, a month later, a year later, ten years later—I'll go back and change a couple of lines and then it works. Some ideas are like that, but other ideas never go anywhere. Some ideas become outdated, but some ideas I can update.
—Robert Davidson, interview with Ian Thom, November 1992

be placed in the College Park development in downtown Toronto. Davidson chose to use the Watchmen to symbolize past, present and future. The interlinked figures suggest communication and a presence in the world while regarding the future. For this complex project, Davidson again assembled a group of assistants and executed an elaborate maquette in yellow cedar. By placing the human figures of the Watchmen on the lowest level of the pole and then again on the top of the largest pole, he confounded traditional iconography, which would place these figures at the top of the pole only. The fact that the group of poles is also conceived of as an ensemble is also unusual. The subtle reappearance of the hat of the central Watchman between the Raven's ears reveals the thought that went into Davidson's conception of the whole. It is a far cry from his earlier additive approach to totem poles as a series of crests piled on each other, seen in the early argillite poles and his first wooden one.[60]

A commission of a different kind was the request to make a talking stick for presentation to Pope John Paul II on the occasion of his 1984 visit to Vancouver *(page 95)*. The only such object that Davidson has produced, it is, in effect, a miniature pole which combines two major Haida crests, Killer Whale and Thunderbird. The execution is startling. Davidson has conceived the Killer Whale as having a huge, pierced dorsal fin and applied a linear pattern to the shaft which is precisely at one with the shape of the talking stick.

That same year, Davidson was also commissioned to produce a bronze for installation in the PepsiCo International Sculpture Park in New York state. Although his first bronze, it is a work of considerable ambition. The design used had first been suggested by the *Frog* of the *Four Circles* prints *(page 61)*, but with the move to three dimensions, Davidson adjusted it. He first explored the three-dimensional idea in a pendant *(page 110)* and then enlarged this to a full-scale wooden model. The bronze and wood versions are unusual in that they are both viewed from above, whereas the pendant is seen vertically. They suggest, in fact, a frog emerging from the water. Davidson chose a rich green patina for the bronze, and the image remains one of his most satisfying.

Although Davidson was busy with these commissions, he did not neglect his studies of Haida ceremony. The Rainbow Creek Dancers were now in great demand for ceremonies both Haida and non-Haida, and he produced masks for them. Among the most striking is that of Gagiit, which Davidson has now essayed several times. Gagiit, a legendary creature of great ugliness, lives on cod, hence the spikes around his mouth. He has never been seen by the Haida people but is one of dwellers in the spirit realm who remind the Haida of their human existence. The mask apparently was always meant to appear at a ceremony but never did. Davidson carved his first Gagiit in 1980, but when he showed it to his grandmother Florence Davidson, she commented that she didn't know that Gagiit was so handsome.[61] Davidson realized that he should try again. An intermediate version *(pages 114–15)* is much more fearsome but still did not satisfy him. The final *Gagiit* mask *(front cover image)*, with unnatural blue-green skin, cod spines, unkempt hair, hawklike nose and grimacing expression, is theatrical and scary, a Gagiit to conjure with and not "too handsome."

Nor did Davidson neglect the art of jewelry; in 1984 he made a series of pendants in gold, abalone and ivory *(page 111)*. This more sculptural jewelry is among his most successful small-scale design. Working from wooden models, he developed final designs noteworthy for their elegance of execution, feeling for materials and sensitivity to form.

Davidson has executed designs on a number of scales, and the best example of this is his *Raven Bringing Light to the World*. Originally an exquisitely carved 1983 pendant of boxwood, gold, ivory and abalone *(page 106)*, the image was subsequently transformed into a huge bronze some 1.2 m (4 feet) across. Davidson has commented that one must be very careful when enlarging an image: "If a line is out a little bit on a maquette, when you blow it up three or four times that line will be out of proportion three or four times."[62] Therefore, his working method is generally to produce a series of interim steps between the initial small-scale idea and the large final version. In the case of *Raven Bringing Light to the World*, the original boxwood pendant was followed by a gold pendant, then a small yellow cedar carving *(back cover image)*, and finally a full-scale red cedar version *(page 107)*. Since the full-scale red cedar version could only be finished to a degree that was still too rough for casting, a plaster version was made and hand-finished as the master for the final bronze. The large bronze, now in the Canadian Museum of Civilization, was gilded; an edition of twelve reduced-scale versions was also cast.

I tried really hard to make a mask to be just hung on the wall, and I couldn't. That mouthpiece always has to be in there. The earlier masks don't have the mouthpiece, because I didn't know about it until later on. But now every mask has the mouthpiece. And they're all intended to be danced. I've tried really hard to not put the mouthpiece in. Even though it doesn't take my time, it takes the apprentice's time, so we go ahead and paint it, then end up saying, "Yeah, put it in. It's part of the mask."

—Robert Davidson, interview with Ian Thom, November 1992

93

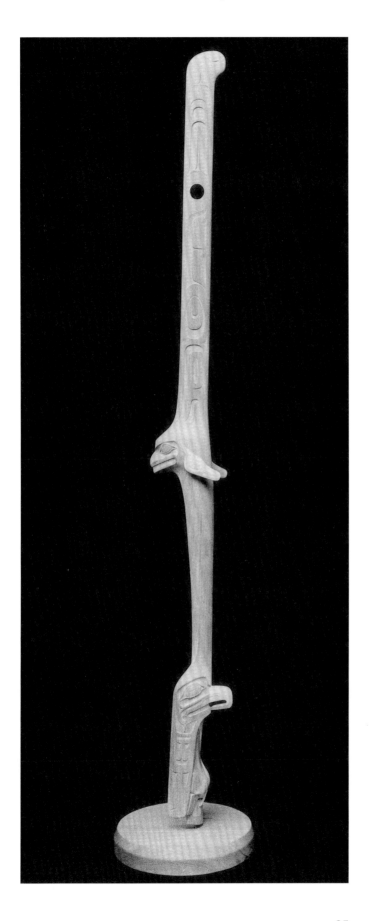

Talking Stick 1984
Yellow cedar
158 x 6.6 x 25.6 cm
COLLECTION OF HIS
HOLINESS JOHN PAUL II.
PHOTO BY ULLI
STELTZER

FACING PAGE:
*Davidson carving the
talking stick, 1984.*
PHOTO BY ULLI
STELTZER

*I was demonstrating,
carving this one* Frog
*soapberry spoon in New
York, and looking at the
shapes that I was using, I
thought: oh that looks
neat, neat to have* Frog
arms coming there and the
Frog *head here. I can still
remember the day I
finished it. I was sitting
outside on the porch. This
was late September, when
fall was coming. Anyway,
I put the* Frog *down. I
was really pleased with it.
This was the evening, and
just as I put it down, a
frog croaked. Ribbet
(mimicking a frog). Like I
finished it and I put it
down. Ribbet. It was
really amazing.*

—Robert Davidson,
interview with Ian Thom,
November 1992

At each step of the enlarging process, Davidson refines his line and proportion. His objects are not, therefore, simply the result of enlarging or reducing an image, but are independently considered works. In this particular piece, however, it is the iconographic conception which is singular. The subject of the Raven bringing light (the sun or moon) to the world is a common one in Northwest Coast art, but usually it is the Raven which is given prominence. Here, the Raven is reduced to head, claws and tail, seemingly incapable of carrying the sun/moon which, at least in gilded form, radiates energy and heat.

Davidson revisited this subject in a charming and unusual painting of 1985 *(page 116)*. He collaborated on it with his daughter, who provided the modified "happy faces," and thus created a whimsical version of this important Haida myth. Raven, by tricking the custodian of the sun, brings a bright yellow ball into the heavens to the delight of humankind, which had, until then, dwelt in the dark. Davidson has commented that he feels Edenshaw was always smiling when he worked,[63] and this image seems to reflect a similar smile on Davidson's part. There is, in fact, often a sense of whimsy and daring in Davidson's work, but never a lack of control. "Every object is an experiment, and marks a progression, but each is contained within a highly stylised system. Ours is a very disciplined art form."[64] This disciplined sense of experiment tempered by humour is seen in objects as diverse as the *Happy Negative Shapes* bracelet *(page 77)*, the elegant *Frog* soapberry spoon *(page 102)* and the pair of images titled *Seven Ravens (page 122)*.[65]

The 1980s saw Davidson move from strength to strength. A second PepsiCo commission, *Three Variations of Killer Whale Myth (pages 108–109)*, is perhaps his most accomplished large-scale statement. The theme of the Killer Whale is woven throughout the fabric of the work, and while the poles may be viewed individually, they become, when seen together, a complex conversation about issues of identity, iconography and sculpture. Sitting in a sculpture park surrounded by the works of Moore, Smith, Lipchitz and others, the poles must function first as form, as sculpture, and yet they are proud symbols of Haida culture. The poles send out a message that the Haida are still here and that Haida culture survives.

In 1984–85, Davidson prepared a maquette *(page 112)* for a possible commission at the Vancouver Aquarium. The subject was again Killer Whale, and he depicted a complex grouping of four Whales which shared two heads and two tails. The maquette has an exceptional sense of movement, with one form smoothly flowing into the other, just as a whale might glide through the water. Davidson visited the aquarium over several months to familiarize himself with the form of the whale and its movements. The carved shapes of the bodies of the Whales are naturalistic, and this verisimilitude is sensitively married to the traditional Haida form vocabulary. Significantly, he left large portions of the wood unadorned, and this fact suggests a life force within the Whales, even as the stylization of the box of Whales would suggest artificiality. The maquette has a grace and power beyond its size, and when one imagines that it was conceived of as being over 3 m (10 feet) in height, the rightness of the artist's conception is apparent. A handsome bronze version, about one quarter size, suggests something of the rhythm that the unrealized larger version would have.

Davidson's recent work has been characterized by a continuing sense of innovation and energy. Whether in a mask such as the *Eagle Spirit (page 144)*, a painting such as *Eagles (page 148)* or *Double Negative (page 155)*, a pole like *Breaking the Totem Barrier (page 99)* or a large-scale carving like *Dorsal Fin (page iii)*, Davidson continues to confound our expectations and push himself forward.[66] Whether in technical innovations, deeper undercutting on a carving (see for example *The Happy Blowhole, page 147*), or iconographic unorthodoxy (as in the almost completely abstract painting *The World Is As Sharp As the Edge of a Knife, page 153*), he sets himself a rigorous standard.

Building upon the bedrock of the past, Robert Davidson's art, reflecting his own growth, speaks to the present and the future. The language is both simple and complex. The rules of Haida design, and his adaptations/extensions of them, inform all of his work, but, as Peter Macnair has noted, there is "a higher level of understanding" and "hidden meanings."[67] Davidson's creations "vibrate out to the viewer,"[68] giving us a glimpse of the spirit world from which all art comes,[69] even as they expand "the circle of knowledge."[70]

All I remember is when I did that, I did the red first and then I did the overlay, and I said, "Ah, I goofed." But I carried on doing it anyway, because I felt really sick about it, having put so much work into it and it didn't work. But after I set it aside for a few days, I got excited about it. I had no idea what I would do. All I knew was that I wanted to do a double negative. This came from my prints, the overlay, and this came from other paintings where I did the ghosting, so the title is Double Negative*, because they're both negatives.*

—Robert Davidson, interview with Ian Thom, November 1992

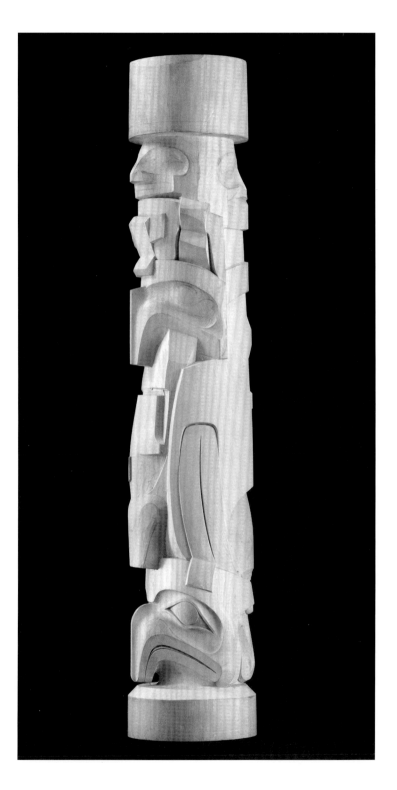

Breaking the Totem
Barrier Maquette
1988–89
Yellow cedar
101.5 cm height, 20 cm
diameter
PRIVATE COLLECTION

FACING PAGE:
Working on Breaking the
Totem Barrier *with Larry
Rosso, 1989.*
PHOTO BY ULLI
STELTZER

SELECTED WORKS

1980–1987

Frog Soapberry Spoon
1980
Yew wood
33.8 x 4.8 x 3.1 cm
PRIVATE COLLECTION

PAGE 100:
Human Mask circa 1980
Red cedar, cedar bark,
acrylic, eagle feathers
77.5 x 25.5 x 10.5 cm
PRIVATE COLLECTION

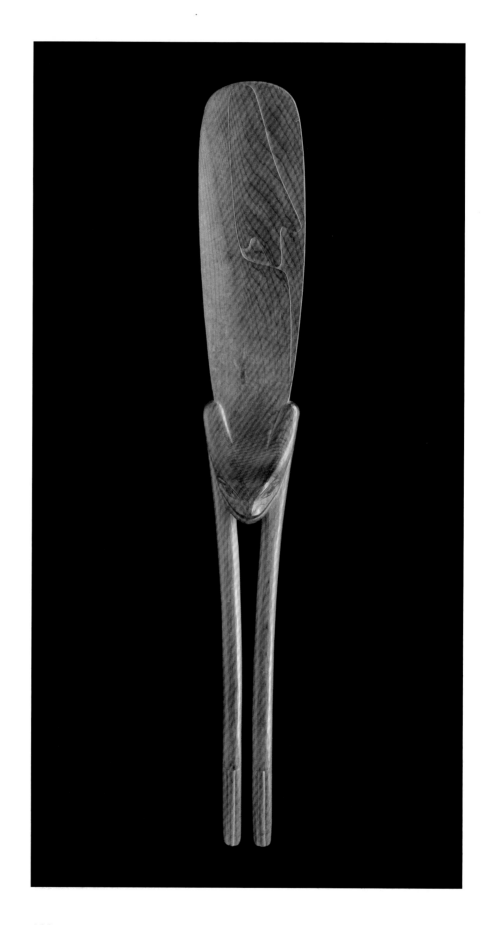

T-Silii-AA-lis (Raven Finned Killer Whale)
1983
Screenprint: black, red on white Arches paper
75.4 x 105.9 cm
PRIVATE COLLECTION

103

Every Year the Salmon
Come Back 1983
Gouache, acrylic
74.5 x 106 cm
PRIVATE COLLECTION

FACING PAGE:
U Is Transforming 1983
Gouache
104.2 x 71.2 cm
PRIVATE COLLECTION

Raven Bringing Light to the World Pendant 1983
Boxwood, gold, abalone, ivory
4.9 cm diameter, 1.9 cm depth
PRIVATE COLLECTION

Frog 1984
Bronze
91.4 cm diameter, 40 cm depth
PRIVATE COLLECTION

FACING PAGE:
Raven Bringing Light to the World 1984
Red cedar
122 cm diameter, 40 cm depth
PRIVATE COLLECTION

Three Variations of Killer
Whale Myth 1984
Yellow cedar, acrylic
a) 136 x 19.9 x 18.5 cm
b) 136.2 x 19.9 x 13.3 cm
c) 130.5 x 19.9 x 12.5 cm
PRIVATE COLLECTION

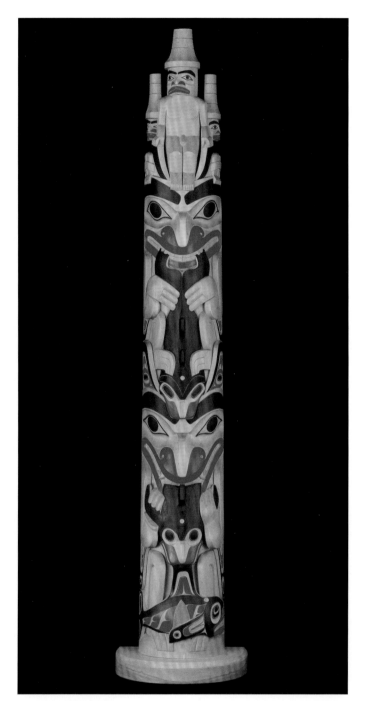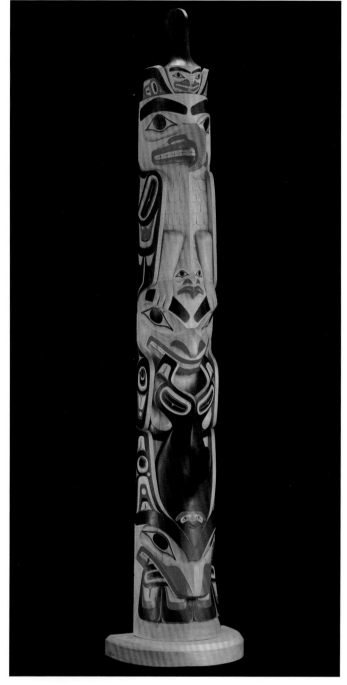

Frog Pendant 1984
Boxwood, abalone, gold,
orange ceramic beads
5.5 cm diameter, 38 cm
length (with beads)
PRIVATE COLLECTION

FACING PAGE:
Moon Pendant 1984
Gold, abalone, ivory
18.3 x 16.9 x 2.2 cm
(with chain)
PRIVATE COLLECTION

Killer Whales Maquette

1984–85

Yellow cedar

16.3 x 25.9 x 27.9 cm

PRIVATE COLLECTION

FACING PAGE:

Dogfish Mask 1985

Alder, acrylic, horsehair,

operculum

31 x 19.9 x 14.8 cm

PRIVATE COLLECTION

Gagiit Mask 1985
Red cedar, alder,
horsehair, hide, acrylic
37 x 37 x 24 cm
THUNDER BAY ART
GALLERY (GIFT OF MR.
C. PEACOCK), 92.1.36

Killer Whale 1985–91
Boxwood
5.5 cm diameter, 2.1 cm
depth
PRIVATE COLLECTION

FACING PAGE:
*Raven Bringing Light to
the World* 1985
Acrylic on paper, with
the assistance of Sara
Davidson
56.8 x 76.4 cm
PRIVATE COLLECTION

Aunt Portrait Mask 1986
Red cedar, acrylic,
feathers, copper,
operculum, horsehair
27.9 x 40.8 x 12.7 cm
PRIVATE COLLECTION

Gagiit Mask 1983
Red cedar, acrylic, bear
fur, musk ox fur, deer
hooves, leather, codfish
spines
64 x 22 x 16cm
PRIVATE COLLECTION

FACING PAGE:
Shark Mask 1986
Red cedar, abalone,
copper, operculum,
horsehair, acrylic
82 x 57.2 x 38 cm
(excluding tail)
PRIVATE COLLECTION

Model Pole 1986

Yellow cedar, acrylic

104 x 24 x 15.5 cm

THUNDER BAY ART
GALLERY (GIFT OF MR.
C. PEACOCK), 92.1.7

FACING PAGE:

Put Your Complaints 'Ere

1987

Gouache

104.1 x 73.7 cm

PRIVATE COLLECTION

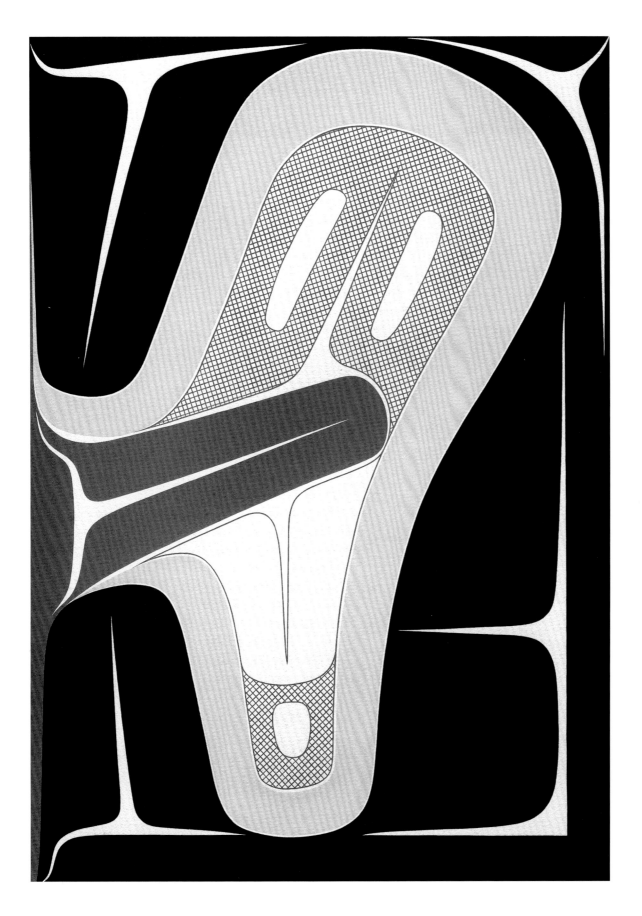

Seven Ravens 1987

One of a set of two prints

Screenprint: blue, red on

ivory Arches paper

56.5 x 55.5 cm

Seven Ravens 1987

One of a set of two prints

Screenprint: blue, red on

ivory Arches paper

56.5 x 55.5 cm

Two Frogs 1987

Acrylic, gouache

48.3 x 102.4 cm

Frog 1968

Red cedar

28.5 x 64.5 x 35 cm

GUUD SAN GLANS

Eagle of the Dawn

by Marianne Jones

The Eagle is my uncle. He is my crest. My concern is to save my uncle's place of dwelling.

—GUUD SAN GLANS (ROBERT DAVIDSON), SPEAKING IN SUPPORT OF EFFORTS TO PREVENT LOGGING ON ATHLI GWAII (LYELL ISLAND) BEFORE THE SUPREME COURT OF BRITISH COLUMBIA, ON 7 NOVEMBER 1985

My name is Jaa-daa Guulx of the Eagle clan, from the village of Skidegate in Haida Gwaii.

When I was a child, my non-Native mother tried very hard to instil in us a sense of pride in our Haida heritage. My Haida father, along with most others of his generation, had been forced through the residential school system, which attempted to strip him of his dignity, language and culture. He survived, with an abhorrence for organized religion and a recurring alcohol problem that further compromised his sense of identity. It would be many years before he told us the Haida stories he had been told. Consequently, my brothers and I gained most of our early cultural knowledge from our visiting Haida grandparents, aunts and cousins—and my mother. She bought books and told us stories and surrounded us with a modest collection of artifacts: an old bentwood box, stone pots found on the beach, a musket from the fur-trading days, cedar baskets, spruce root baskets and two small masks. Obviously carved for the tourist trade, these masks had been produced by young and inexperienced carvers as learning pieces. So my first memory of traditional masks was of rough and inert objects. In the back of my mind, however, was always the knowledge that masks were not meant just to hang on walls. It was not right, and did not do the masks justice.

I first came to know Guud San Glans when I was invited to join Tuul Gundlaas Xyaal Xaada (the Rainbow Creek Dancers) in 1984. The group

Before I was born, they did away with all the totem poles, just one standing by the road, a great big one. I saw a few others, too, but I don't remember where. The minister came around and made everyone cut all the totem poles down and burn them. Some houses had three totem poles. The minister called it "their gods." But it is not, it's to let the descendants know who they are. They didn't want to marry their own clans. That's why they had crests on the poles. Eagle clan and Raven clan are supposed to marry, not Eagle clan to Eagle clan.
—Florence Davidson, quoted in *Robes of Power: Totem Poles on Cloth* by Doreen Jensen and Polly Sargent

was formed in 1980 by Robert with the help of his brother Reg and Robert's wife-to-be, Dorothy Grant.

When he was a young man, Robert moved from the village of Massett in Haida Gwaii to Vancouver to attend high school. People were curious about him. They asked him where he had come from, and what it meant to be Haida. Those questions inspired Robert to visit museums and to study art and photographs that opened up a world he knew little about. It was the world of his ancestors, and when he returned to Haida Gwaii to visit, he wanted to celebrate that world with his village. He decided to carve a pole and to raise that pole in the village of Massett.

I think Robert's visits to museums as a young man were similar to my experiences as a child. In the same way that I knew that masks were not meant just to hang on walls, Robert understood the insufficiency of the Western way of displaying art. He knew that a pole, once carved, would be brought to life by the ceremony around its raising. In this way, the raising of the *Bear Mother* pole in 1969, and the potlatch that took place, became what Robert calls "a medium for transferring knowledge." In preparation for these events, he asked his elders for advice. His Naanii (Grandmother, Florence) and Tsinii (Grandfather, Robert Sr.) were among those who gathered to help prepare for the first pole raising in Massett in almost fifty years.

Many meetings were held, and all discussions were in the Haida language. Like many of his generation, Robert spoke almost no Haida. Eddie Jones translated the words of Eliza Abrahams, Amanda Edgars, Timothy Edgars, Emily White (Naanii's sister), Grace Wilson, Augustus Wilson, Ida Smith, Lucy Frank, Peter Hill and Elija Jones. The elders practised songs, and Naanii and Tsinii instigated a dance practice. Because they had no masks, Naanii sent someone to get a brown paper bag and cut holes for the eyes. Robert recorded the elders' practice sessions and listened to the tapes of his grandfather to hear the melody. He sang the first of many songs to Naanii at the family fish camp at the Yakoun River, and she worked with him on his pronunciation.

Then as now, Robert was absorbing information from a number of sources. He was perfecting his art and his carving skills, and he was also looking to his community for direction. People told him that because he is of the Eagle clan, he should put an Eagle at the top of the pole. Robert felt

126

that the pole was for everyone in the village, not for one person or one clan. Even then, as he was listening and learning, Robert was redefining tradition. This belief in the integrity of cultural tradition and the ability to move tradition forward is the hallmark of Robert's work.

Within our cultural spaces, Robert's work is more than "art," more than objects with a monetary value in the commercial art market. At a feast or a potlatch, his work is an integral part of ceremony, and because of this, we view and perceive his work in an entirely different way.

Even though there is no word for "art" in the Haida language, our artforms are strongly connected to our spirituality and philosophies. This is the case for many First Nations. In a display at the 1992 exhibition entitled "Pathways of Tradition" at the National Museum of the American Indian in New York, Conrad House, a Navajo, explains: "We have no word for art, we have no word for religion. Because there is no need . . . to separate those concepts away from our real life. Because real life has all that . . . How you live is an art . . . How you go about is a religion."

Robert says that our artforms link the spirit world with this world. Both are inspired, sustained and nourished by Haida Gwaii, our homeland, which provides us with wood to carve poles, canoes and masks; cedar bark and spruce roots to make hats; shells to adorn masks and button blankets, and food for feasts and potlatches. Those poles, button blankets and regalia bearing images of clan and/or family crests are public affirmations of our traditional identity. An essential element of Haida cultural events (potlatches, feasts, pole raisings, name givings and adoptions) is the participation of family, clan and community, because traditional identity *must* be publicly displayed and witnessed.

Haida cultural continuity was disrupted by many outside influences. The smallpox epidemic of 1862 decimated whole villages almost overnight. Within fifty years, 88 per cent of the population was lost to smallpox, measles, influenza and a host of other diseases. Disease, the imposition of the Indian Act (which prohibited the potlatch in 1884), and the impact of residential schools, combined with the influence of Christianity, created a historical gap that our generation is now attempting to bridge.

For a time, the evolution of Northwest Coast First Nations traditions was forced into dormancy. That time has passed. Once again the creation

The first Eagle headdress I carved didn't fit on anybody's head. It wasn't until I learned how to dance that I understood the art. Next time I did an Eagle headpiece, it had a purpose; it could fit on a person's head and be used for dancing. It wasn't heavy like the first one either. You can get a headache if you dance with all that weight on your head. . . . So when I started to dance I had to make it up, just to imitate the animals I was portraying. At first they didn't tell me much more than what I was doing wrong. There was Nonnie and a couple of older people sitting around when we had dance practice. "You just don't dance like women do with their hands on their hips." That's what they said, and they bawled me out. Later, when we danced and we were doing it right . . . they said, "That's how it is, you do it that way!"

—Reg Davidson, quoted in *A Haida Potlatch* by Ulli Steltzer

of ceremonial objects nurtures the need for ceremony. Poles need to be raised. Masks invite dancers to flesh out their characters. Blankets live after being danced the first time. Old songs are sung, new ones are composed in the Haida language. The resurrection of ceremony validates the role that tradition plays in our contemporary lives and reinforces our cultural view of the "life" of these inanimate objects. The objects that Western culture calls "art," we see born through ceremony.

Adaptation has always been a part of Haida culture and art, and there are many examples of this. Songs and dances are exchanged as signs of esteem, peace and friendship. As sea otter robes evolved into button blankets, pearl buttons took the place of dentalia and abalone shells. Gold and silver bracelets replaced the tattoos of family crests on high-ranking Haida because Christians found them unacceptable. Some songs and dances survived the historical gap created by the Indian Act and the influence of Christianity. While Robert and Tuul Gundlaas Xyaal Xaada perform many of these old songs and dances, Robert has composed a number of new songs and dances in the traditional style. The integrity and authenticity, in both form and content, of these new songs and dances shows that adaptation is still part of Haida culture.

PRAYER SONG

waii.aad t'laau gam tajaau dii sgwaii 7aat'awonggaa
waii.aad t'laau gam tajaau dii sgwaii 7aat'awonggaa

(today there is no wind to push me)

waii.aad t'laau gam tajawee xanggaa hlkanggaa
waii.aad t'laau gam tajawee xanggaa hlkanggaa

(today there is no wind to hold me back)

waii.aad t'laau dagwii gan gahls swgan t'lang kwaagiidang
waii.aad t'laau dagwii gan gahls swgan t'lang kwaagiidang

(today we will go on our own strength)

—Robert Davidson, 1984

128

We dance for many reasons and in many places. We celebrated with Bill Reid the launching and homecoming of the canoe *Loo Taas*, pole raisings for Jim Hart, a canoe launching and pole raisings for Reg Davidson. We are honoured to attend feasts, potlatches and memorials for chiefs and elders at home in Haida Gwaii and in other First Nations villages and territories. We dance in support of our political goals for the Council of the Haida Nation and other First Nations people. In these larger settings, Tuul Gundlaas Xyaal Xaada identify our people, our land and our nation.

In 1989, Robert assumed the responsibility of principal host of an ongoing annual event at the Yakoun River and in the village of Old Massett, the celebration that marks the return of the first salmon. For this occasion, Robert created a new mask, song and dance. The *Salmon* mask has since danced in many communities. It is used to represent and acknowledge the shared respect, importance and spiritual nature of the return of the salmon to all Haida and Northwest Coast First Nations people.

In writing for his 1992 Vancouver exhibit, *A Voice from the Inside*, Robert said: "Since the almost complete destruction of our spirit, the disconnection of our values and beliefs, it has been the art that brought us back to our roots." There is no better illustration of this than the mask, song and dance which honour the return of the salmon. As art invites ceremony, so too do events like the salmon ceremony inspire art. I believe Haida art and culture to be inextricably intertwined; knowledge of either one enhances understanding of the other.

For me, traditional dancing has been a journey into my own identity, both as a Haida and as a performing artist. One of the first requirements for all dancers is making and acquiring regalia. When I started, I sought the help of my aunts, and they told me what crest should be on my button blanket. Robert offered the use of a suitable design; Dorothy helped me choose the materials and showed me how to cut the Hummingbird which identifies me when I dance. Learning Haida songs, and consequently a little of the Haida language, has enriched this journey, because the language was so effectively removed from our generation.

Robert's commitment to share knowledge and innovation in song and ceremony contributes to contemporary Haida culture. The most important reason to dance lives in the smiles of our elders and the faces of the children who jostle for the best view. Through Tuul Gundlaas Xyaal

Xaada and other dance groups in Haida Gwaii and Alaska, Haida children will inherit more than masks that hang on walls. They will be part of a dynamic culture and compelling ceremonial tradition.

> *We, the elders of the future, are . . . once again instigating potlatches, songs, and dances based on our traditional roots, and by the inspiration to keep tradition moving, creating new songs, dances, and rituals . . . the Haida have come full circle.*
> —El-Ski-Di (Dorothy Grant), Kaigaani of the Raven clan, quoted in *Robes of Power: Totem Poles on Cloth* by Doreen Jensen and Polly Sargent

SELECTED WORKS

1988–Present

Dawning of the Eagle Too
Mask 1989
Red cedar, acrylic,
graphite, feathers, hair
33 x 25.4 x 20.3 cm
PRIVATE COLLECTION

132

Rock Scallops 1988

Gouache

73 x 103.9 cm

Portrait of an Eagle
Transforming 1988–89
Acrylic, gouache
103.7 x 73.4 cm
PRIVATE COLLECTION

Southeast Wind and Foam
Woman 1989
Screenprint: blue, red on
white Arches paper
101.6 x 101.4 cm
PRIVATE COLLECTION

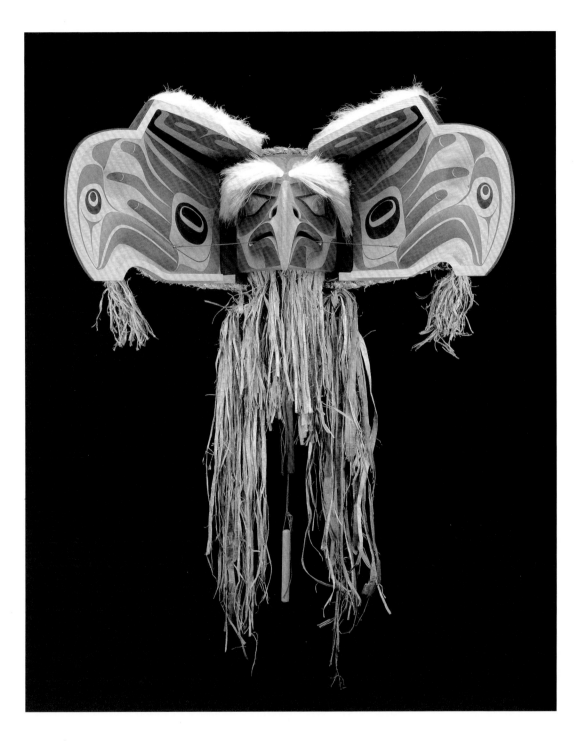

Eagle Transforming into Itself 1990
Closed and open views
Red cedar, acrylic, goat hair, operculum, cedar bark
121.9 x 91.4 x 55.8 cm
COLLECTION OF STUART O. MCLAUGHLIN, GROUSE MOUNTAIN RESORTS LTD., NORTH VANCOUVER

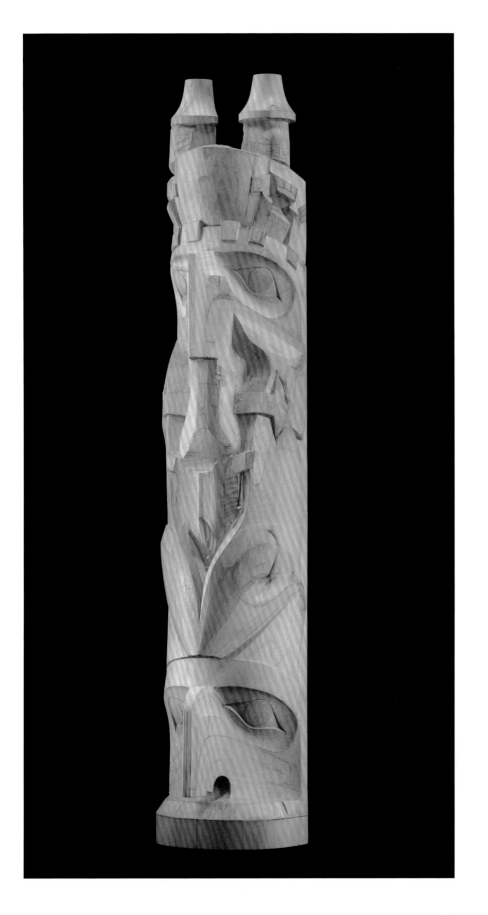

Two Eagles (The Inside Job) Maquette 1990
Yellow cedar
86.7 x 17.6 x 14.5 cm
PRIVATE COLLECTION

FACING PAGE:
Salmon Mask 1990
Red cedar, operculum,
acrylic, cedar bark, cloth
55 x 38 x 66 cm
(excluding tail)
PRIVATE COLLECTION

Thunderbird and Killer Whale Bracelet 1990
Gold (22 carat)
5.6 x 6.6 x 6.2 cm
PRIVATE COLLECTION

FACING PAGE:
Sgan Mask 1990
Red cedar, cedar bark,
acrylic, feathers,
operculum
30 x 25 x 17 cm
PRIVATE COLLECTION

Moon Pendant 1990
Gold, abalone, ivory
(no chain)
4.5 x 4 x 0.3 cm
PRIVATE COLLECTION

FACING PAGE:
Wolf Drum 1991
Deerskin, antler, rawhide,
acrylic
61.6 cm diameter,
7.2 cm depth
PRIVATE COLLECTION

Thunderbird Panel 1992
Red cedar
136.5 x 232.4 x 4.6 cm
GALLERY OF TRIBAL
ART, VANCOUVER

FACING PAGE:
Eagle Spirit Mask 1991
Red cedar, acrylic,
operculum, cedar bark,
brass, goat hair
25.4 x 38.1 x 25.4 cm
PRIVATE COLLECTION

The Happy Blowhole 1992

Yellow cedar

37.5 cm diameter, 17.8
cm depth

VANCOUVER ART
GALLERY
(VAG ACQUISITION
FUND), VAG 92.50

FACING PAGE:

Killer Whale 1992

Bronze

37.5 cm diameter,

17.8 cm depth

PRIVATE COLLECTION

Eagle Transforming 1991
Screenprint: blue, green,
red on white Arches
paper
104.1 x 107 cm
PRIVATE COLLECTION

FACING PAGE:
Eagles 1991
Gouache, watercolour
101.6 x 101.6 cm
GALLERY OF TRIBAL
ART, VANCOUVER

149

Sea Wolf and Killer Whales 1992
Watercolour, gouache
101.6 x 73.7 cm
PRIVATE COLLECTION

FACING PAGE:
Wolf Mask 1992
Red cedar, operculum,
copper, acrylic, cedar
bark, eagle feathers
31.8 x 20.3 x 26.7 cm
PRIVATE COLLECTION

*Raven Bringing Light to
the World* Drum 1992
Deerskin, wood, acrylic
60.9 cm diameter
PRIVATE COLLECTION

FACING PAGE:
*The World Is As Sharp As
the Edge of a Knife* 1992
Watercolour, gouache
73.7 x 101.6 cm
PRIVATE COLLECTION

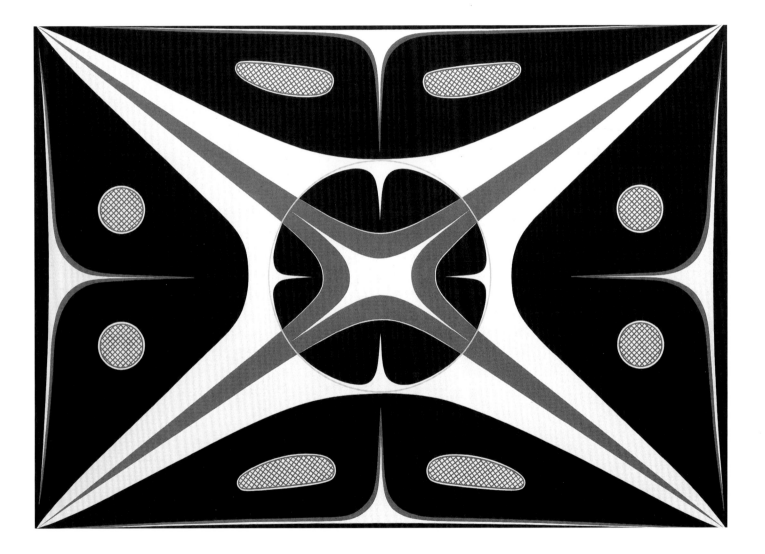

Double Negative 1992

Gouache, watercolour

73.7 x 101.6 cm

NOTES TO THE

ESSAYS

Notes to "Traders of Tradition: The History of Haida Art"

I wish to thank Robert Davidson for his gracious assistance on this paper. Others who read earlier drafts of this work and made extremely useful comments are Margaret Blackman, Janet Catherine Berlo, Bill Holm, Alan Hoover, Gene Lebovics, Peter Macnair and Ruth Phillips.

1 For other major works on Robert Davidson, see Marjorie Halpin, *Cycles: The Graphic Art of Robert Davidson*, Museum Note no. 7 (Vancouver: University of British Columbia Museum of Anthropology, 1979); Alan Hoover, "Innovation in Contemporary Haida Art: The Bracelets of Robert Davidson" (Paper presented at the eighth biennial conference of the Native American Art Studies Association, Sioux Falls, South Dakota, 1991); Hilary Stewart, *Robert Davidson, Haida Printmaker* (Vancouver/Toronto: Douglas & McIntyre, 1979).

2 Marcia Crosby, in her essay "Construction of the Imaginary Indian" in *Vancouver Anthropology: The Institutional Politics of Art*, ed. Stan Douglas (Vancouver: Talonbooks, 1991), 279-87, asserts that seeing Bill Reid as a heroic reviver of a dying culture is part of a larger self-referential process on the part of whites that stereotypes and objectifies Native people.

3 This kind of evaluation appeared early in the literature on Native art. Franz Boas, in his discussion of Chilkat blankets, "Notes on the Blanket Designs" in George T. Emmons, "The Chilkat Blanket," *American Museum of Natural History Memoirs* 3 (1907):351-400, mentions and then disregards the more

contemporary versions of these textiles because on them the formal conventions of the classic blankets are "dismantled." And, in *Primitive Art* (Oslo: Institutet for Sammenlignende Kulturforskning, 1927), 144, Boas refers to the influence of European wares on Native art as "contamination." It is worth noting, however, that despite this, Boas does use what we could categorize as arts of acculturation—models of totem poles, silver bracelets, and argillite carvings—alongside more "traditional" carvings, as examples in his analysis of Northwest Coast art in *Primitive Art*.

I discuss Boas's complicated relationship to acculturated art in "Franz Boas, John Swanton, and the New Haida Sculpture at the American Museum of Natural History" in *The Early Years of Native American Art History: The Politics of Scholarship and Collecting*, ed. J. Berlo (Seattle: University of Washington Press, 1992) and in *A Wealth of Thought: Franz Boas on Native American Art* (Seattle: University of Washington Press; Vancouver/Toronto: Douglas & McIntyre, in press).

4 Margaret Blackman, "Creativity in Acculturation: Art, Architecture and Ceremony from the Northwest Coast," *Ethnohistory* 23 (1976):389.

5 Blackman goes on to point out that among anthropologists, only Frederica de Laguna and Philip Drucker treated late contact cultures as equally authentic as earlier ones; Wayne Suttles, Wilson Duff and Michael Kew should be included in this category.

6 See Knut R. Fladmark, Kenneth M. Ame and Patricia D. Sutherland, "Prehistory of the Northern Coast of British Columbia" in *Handbook of North American Indians,* Vol. 7, *Northwest*

Coast (Washington, D.C.: Smithsonian Institution Press, 1990), 229-39, for a brief summary of northern British Columbia coast prehistory.

7 It would be erroneous to consider the movement of influences only from non-Natives to Natives. In a suggestive study, Nicholas Thomas, *Entangled Objects: Exchange, Material Culture, and Colonialism in the Pacific* (Cambridge, Mass.: Harvard University Press, 1991), analyses the reciprocal relationships that native peoples in the Pacific established with their colonizers.

8 Margaret B. Blackman, "Continuity and Change in Northwest Coast Ceremonialism: Introduction," *Arctic Anthropology* 14 (1977):2.

9 Blackman here introduces a series of papers given at the 1974 American Anthropological Association meeting in Mexico City on "Continuity and Change in Northwest Coast Ceremonialism." The symposium participants included Pamela Amoss, Margaret Blackman, Philip Drucker, William Elmendorf, Bill Holm, Susan Kenyon, Mary Lee Stearns, and Wayne Suttles.

10 For the timelessness of much of the discourse on native peoples, see Johannes Fabian, *Time and the Other: How Anthropology Makes Its Object* (New York: Columbia University Press, 1983). For Native responses to the representation of their "disappearance," see Deborah Doxtoder, "The Home of Indian Culture and Other Stories for the Museum," *Muse* 6 (1988):26-31; Karen Duffek and Tom Hill, *Beyond History* (Vancouver: Vancouver Art Gallery, 1989); Gerald McMaster and Lee-Ann Martin, "Introduction" in *Indigena: Contemporary Native Perspectives*, ed. McMaster and Martin (Vancouver/Toronto: Douglas & McIntyre, 1992), 11-23; Alfred Young Man, "The Metaphysics of North American Indian Art" in McMaster and Martin, *Indigena*, 81-99.

11 For readings on colonial and postcolonial discourse, see K. Anthony Appiah, "Is the Post- in Postmodernism the Post- in Postcolonial?" *Critical Inquiry* 17 (1991):336-57; Talal Asad, "Afterword: From the History of Colonial Anthropology to the

Anthropology of Western Hegemony" in *Colonial Situations: Essays on the Contextualization of Ethnographic Knowledge*, History of Anthropology Vol. 7, ed. George Stocking (Madison: University of Wisconsin Press, 1991), 314-24; Homi Bhabha, "Of Mimicry and Man: The Ambivalence of Colonial Discourse," *October* 28 (1984):125-33 and "Postcolonial Authority and Postmodern Guilt" in *Cultural Studies*, ed. L. Grossberg, C. Nelson, P. Treichler (New York/London: Routledge, 1992), 56-65; John and Jean Comaroff, *Ethnography and the Historical Imagination* (Boulder: Westview Press, 1992); Annie E. Coombes, "Ethnography and the Formation of National and Cultural Identities" in *The Myth of Primitivism: Perspectives on Art*, ed. S. Hiller (London/New York: Routledge, 1991), 189-214; R. Ferguson, M. Gever, T. T. Minh-ha, C. West, eds., *Out There: Marginalization and Contemporary Cultures* (New York/Cambridge, Mass: Museum of Contemporary Art and MIT Press, 1990); P. Mariani and J. Crary, "In the Shadow of the West: Edward Said" in *Discourses: Conversations in Postmodern Art and Culture,* ed. R. Ferguson, W. Olander, M. Tucker, K. Fiss (New York/Cambridge, Mass: Museum of Contemporary Art and MIT Press, 1990), 93-104; Edward Said, *Orientalism* (New York: Vintage Books, 1979); G. C. Spivak, *The Post-Colonial Critic: Interviews, Strategies, Dialogues*, ed. S. Harasym (New York/London: Routledge, 1990); George Stocking, "Colonial Situations" in *Colonial Situations*, 3-8.

12 Guy Brett, "Unofficial Versions" in *The Myth of Primitivism,* 116.

13 This essay has benefited from the theoretical writings of scholars sometimes labelled as "postmodernists," including David Harvey, *The Condition of Postmodernity* (Cambridge: Basil Blackwell, Inc., 1989); Frederic Jameson, *Postmodernism, or, The Cultural Logic of Late Capitalism* (Durham: Duke University Press, 1991); Charles Jencks, "Postmodern vs. Late Modern" in *Zeitgeist in Babel: The Postmodern Controversy*, ed. I.

Hoesterey (Bloomington: Indiana University Press, 1991), 4-21. See also Charles Jencks, ed., *The Post-Modern Reader* (New York: St. Martin's Press, 1992); Jeffrey C. Alexander and Steven Seidman, eds., *Culture and Society: Contemporary Debates* (Cambridge: Cambridge University Press, 1990).

For interesting literature on representations of culture as well as anthropological discourse, see Lila Abu-Lughod, "Writing Against Culture" in *Recapturing Anthropology: Working in the Present*, ed. R. Fox (Santa Fe: School of American Research Press, 1991); Paul Atkinson, *The Ethnographic Imagination: Textual Constructions of Reality* (New York/London: Routledge, 1990); James Clifford, *The Predicament of Culture: Twentieth-Century Ethnography, Literature and Art* (Cambridge, Mass: Harvard University Press, 1988); James Clifford and George E. Marcus, eds., *Writing Culture: The Poetics and Politics of Ethnography* (Berkeley: University of California Press, 1986); Virginia Dominguez, "Of Other Peoples: Beyond the 'Salvage Paradigm'" in *Dia Art Foundation Discussions in Contemporary Culture* no. 1, ed. H. Foster (Seattle: Bay Press, 1987, 131-37 and "Invoking Culture: The Messy Side of 'Cultural Politics,'" *South Atlantic Quarterly* 91 (1992):19-42; Richard G. Fox, "For a Nearly New Culture History" in *Recapturing Anthropology: Working in the Present*, ed. R. Fox (Santa Fe: School of American Research, 1991), 93-114; Arnold Krupat, "Irony in Anthropology: The Work of Franz Boas" in *Modernist Anthropology: From Fieldwork to Text*, ed. M. Manganaro (Princeton: Princeton University Press, 1990), 133-45 and *Ethnocriticism: Ethnography, History, Literature* (Berkeley: University of California Press, 1992); Adam Kuper, *The Invention of Primitive Society: Transformations of an Illusion* (New York/London: Routledge, 1988); Robin Ridington, *Trail to Heaven: Knowledge and Narrative in a Northern Native Community* (Iowa City: University of Iowa Press; Vancouver/Toronto, Douglas & McIntyre, 1988); Renato Rosaldo, *Culture and Truth: The Remaking of Social Analysis* (Boston:

Beacon Press, 1989).

14 Robert T. Boyd, "Demographic History, 1774-1874" in *Handbook of North American Indians,* 136.

15 For summaries of the literature on Haida history and ethnology, see Douglas Cole and David Darling, "History of the Early Period" in *Handbook of North American Indians*, 119-34; Michael Kew, "History of Coastal British Columbia Since 1849" in *Handbook of North American Indians*, 159-68; Margaret B. Blackman, "Haida Traditional Culture" in *Handbook of North American Indians*, 240-60.

16 Charles Pierre Claret de Fleurieu, *A Voyage Around the World Performed During the Years 1790, 1791, and 1792, by Etienne Marchand* (London: T. N. Longmans and O. Rees, 1801), 281.

17 Johan Adrian Jacobsen, *Alaskan Voyage, 1881-1883: An Expedition to the Northwest Coast of America*, trans. E. Gunther (Chicago: University of Chicago Press, 1977), 17-18. Peter Macnair (personal communication to the author, 1992) points out that it is not clear how many totem poles produced by "mainland tribes" Jacobsen actually saw.

18 Bill Holm, "Art" in *Handbook of North American Indians*, 605. Along with the Tsimshian and Tlingit, the Haida had developed the exquisite northern formline style. In the Northwest Coast chapter of his classic book published in 1927, *Primitive Art*, Franz Boas credits the northern Tlingit, Tsimshian, and Haida with originating the style we now term formline. Philip Drucker, *Cultures of the North Pacific Coast* (San Francisco: Chandler, 1965), 154, credits the Haida with a strong influence on Kwakwaka'wakw art at the turn of the century. Wilson Duff, *Arts of the Raven: Masterworks by the Northwest Coast Indian* (Vancouver: Vancouver Art Gallery, 1967) characterizes the Haida as "the most intensely artistic" of the Northwest Coast peoples.

19 Although the Haida moved from their villages to larger communities, they never actually abandoned those sites but returned regularly to them for seasonal food-gathering activities.

20 According to late nineteenth-century documents, the Haida seem to have been willing participants in this

acculturative process. In the 1870s, after the Haida asked the missionaries in Metlakatla why none had been sent to Haida Gwaii, the Anglican missionary William H. Collison was sent to Massett. By the request of the Haida themselves, school classes, church services, and meetings were conducted in English.

For more on this, see Douglas Cole, *Captured Heritage: The Scramble for Northwest Coast Artifacts* (Vancouver/ Toronto: Douglas & McIntyre; Seattle: University of Washington Press, 1985); Douglas Cole and Ira Chaikin, *An Iron Hand Upon the People: The Law Against the Potlatch on the Northwest Coast* (Vancouver/Toronto: Douglas & McIntyre; Seattle: University of Washington Press, 1990), 56-59; Margaret B. Blackman, *Windows on the Past: The Photographic Ethnohistory of the Northern and Kaigani Haida*, National Museum of Man Mercury Series, Canadian Ethnology Service Paper no. 74 (Ottawa: National Museums of Canada, 1981), 20-32; Robin Fisher, *Contact and Conflict: Indian-European Relations in British Columbia, 1774-1890* (Vancouver: University of British Columbia Press, 1977); Wilson Duff, *The Indian History of British Columbia, Vol. 1: The Impact of the White Man*, Anthropology in British Columbia Memoirs no. 5 (Victoria: British Columbia Provincial Museum, 1964); Carol Sheehan, *Pipes That Won't Smoke, Coal That Won't Burn: Haida Sculpture in Argillite* (Calgary, Alberta: Glenbow Museum, 1981), 44-55.

21 Aldona Jonaitis, *From the Land of the Totem Poles: The Northwest Coast Indian Art Collection at the American Museum of Natural History* (Seattle: University of Washington Press; Vancouver/Toronto: Douglas & McIntyre, 1988), 197-201.

22 John Swanton to Franz Boas, 30 September 1900. Anthropology Department Archives, American Museum of Natural History, New York.

23 John Swanton, "Contributions to the Ethnology of the Haida," *American Museum of Natural History Memoirs* 8 (1905):1-300.

24 Margaret B. Blackman, *Windows on the Past*, 2. Some of my own earlier work

was informed by this salvage paradigm: *Art of the Northern Tlingit* (Seattle: University of Washington Press; Vancouver/Toronto: Douglas & McIntyre, 1986). Further thought, inspired greatly by contemporary movements in literary criticism and anthropology, has brought a new perspective on these issues.

25 Sheehan, *Pipes That Won't Smoke*, 15.

26 Blackman, "Creativity in Acculturation," 87-413.

27 Margaret B. Blackman, "Totems to Tombstones: Culture Change As Viewed Through the Haida Mortuary Complex," *Ethnology* 12 (1973):47-56.

28 Jacobsen, *Alaskan Voyage*, 17.

29 The scholarship on Haida argillite chronology is extensive. While a detailed analysis of this literature is beyond the scope of this paper, the reader is directed to Alan Hoover's thoughtful review of that literature in his "Appendix: A History of the Study of Argillite Carving" in Peter Macnair and Alan Hoover, *The Magic Leaves: A History of Argillite Carving* (Victoria: British Columbia Provincial Museum, 1984) 201-7, based in large part on Macnair's analysis. Works subjected to their careful scrutiny include Marius Barbeau, *Haida Carvers in Argillite*, National Museum of Canada Bulletin 139, Anthropological Series 38 (Ottawa: National Museum of Canada, 1957); Carole Kaufmann, "Functional Aspects of Haida Argillite Carvings" in *Ethnic and Tourist Arts: Cultural Expressions from the Fourth World*, ed. N. Graburn (Berkeley: University of California Press, 1976), 56-69; Leslie Drew and Douglas Wilson, *Argillite: Art of the Haida* (North Vancouver, B.C.: Hancock House, 1980); Sheehan, *Pipes That Won't Smoke*.

Other notable works on this subject include Robin Wright's extensive publications: "Haida Argillite Ship Pipes," *American Indian Art* 5 (1979):40-47; "Haida Argillite Pipes: The Influence of Clay Pipes," *American Indian Art* 5 (1980):42-47, 88; "Haida Argillite— Made for Sale," *American Indian Art* 8 (1982):48-55; "Anonymous Attributions: A Tribute to a Mid-19th Century Haida Argillite Pipe Carver, the Master of the

Long Fingers" in *The Box of Daylight*, ed. Bill Holm (Seattle: Seattle Art Museum and University of Washington Press, 1983), 139-42; *Nineteenth-Century Haida Argillite Pipe Carvers: Stylistic Attributions* (Ph.D. dissertation, University of Washington, 1985); "Haida Argillite Carving in the Sheldon Jackson Museum" in *Faces, Voices, and Dreams: A Celebration of the Centennial of the Sheldon Jackson Museum*, ed. Peter Corey (Sitka: Sheldon Jackson Museum, 1987), 76-99.

30 Major J. W. Powell, quoted in Cole, *Captured Heritage*, 292. The characterization of whites as "the higher race" was typical of the late nineteenth century. Franz Boas's anthropology was based in large measure on his ultimately successful efforts to dispel the notion of a hierarchy of races and prove the equality of all human beings. See George Stocking, *Race, Culture and Evolution: Essays in the History of Anthropology* (Chicago: University of Chicago Press, 1968) and *A Franz Boas Reader: The Shaping of American Anthropology, 1883-1911* (Chicago: University of Chicago Press, 1974); Jonaitis, *A Wealth of Thought*.

31 Swanton, "Contributions to the Ethnology of the Haida," 122-54.

32 "Franz Boas, John Swanton, and the New Haida Sculpture" in *The Early Years of Native American Art History*, 22-61.

33 Wolfgang Paalen, "Totem Art," *Dyn* 4-5 (1943):19. For more on the Surrealists and Northwest Coast art, see Elizabeth Cowling, "The Eskimos, the American Indians, and the Surrealists," *Art History* 1 (1978):484-500 and Aldona Jonaitis, "Creations of Mystics and Philosophers: The White Man's Perceptions of Northwest Coast Indian Art from the 1930s to the Present," *American Indian Culture and Research Journal* 5 (1981): 1-48.

For more on Paalen and Northwest Coast art, see Amy Winter, "The Germanic Reception of Native American Art: Wolfgang Paalen as Collector, Scholar and Artist," *European Review of Native American Studies* 6 (1992):17-26.

34 Frederic Douglas and Rene d'Harnoncourt, *Indian Art of the United States* (New York: Museum of Modern Art, 1941), 168.

35 Marius Barbeau, *Haida Myths Illustrated in Argillite Carvings*, National Museum of Canada Bulletin 127, Anthropological Series 32 (Ottawa: National Museum of Canada, 1953) and *Haida Carvers in Argillite*. Barbeau's publications suffer from occasional lapses into sloppy scholarship such as erroneous attributions.

36 Barbeau, *Haida Carvers in Argillite*, iii.

37 Duff, *Arts of the Raven*; Peter Macnair, Alan Hoover and Kevin Neary, *The Legacy: Continuing Traditions of Canadian Northwest Coast Indian Art* (Victoria: British Columbia Provincial Museum, 1980); Bill Holm, *Spirit and Ancestor: A Century of Northwest Coast Art at the Burke Museum* (Seattle: University of Washington Press, 1983); Jonaitis, *From the Land of the Totem Poles*.

38 Ruth Phillips, "Why Not Tourist Art?: Significant Silences in Native American Museum Representation" in *After Colonialism: Imperialism and the Colonial Aftermath*, ed. Gyan Prakash (Princeton: Princeton University Press, 1993).

39 Peter Macnair (personal communication to the author, 1992), makes the following statement about the nature of Haida argillite carving and its relationship to the formline system: "About 80% of Haida argillite is essentially sculptural, with correct but minimal formline decoration as wing and fin design. It is not until the 1880s, and with primarily Edenshaw's influence, that we find any serious exploration of fully developed formline design."

40 For interesting discussions of the reception of other Native art made for sale, see Ruth B. Phillips: "What is 'Huron Art'?": Native American Art and the New Art History," *Canadian Journal of Native Studies* 9 (1989):167-91; "Glimpses of Eden: Iconographic Themes in Huron Pictorial Tourist Art," *European Review of Native American Studies* 5 (1991):19-28; "Why Not Tourist Art?" in *After Colonialism*.

See also Molly Lee, "Appropriating the Primitive: Turn-of-the-Century Collection and Display of Native

Alaskan Art," *Arctic Anthropology* 28 (1991):6-15; Trudy Nicks, *The Creative Tradition: Indian Handicrafts and Tourist Art* (Edmonton, Alberta: Provincial Museum of Alberta, 1982).

For more on the general topic of "tourist art," see Nelson Graburn, *Ethnic and Tourist Arts: Cultural Expressions from the Fourth World* (Berkeley: University of California Press, 1976).

For more on tourism itself, see Dean MacCannell, *The Tourist: A New Theory of the Leisure Class* (New York: Schocken Books, 1976) and *Empty Meeting Grounds: The Tourist Papers* (New York/London: Routledge, 1992). See also James Clifford, "Traveling Cultures" in *Cultural Studies*, 96-111; Mary Louise Pratt, *Imperial Eyes: Travel Writing and Transculturation* (New York/London: Routledge, 1992).

41 For more on commoditization, see Igor Kopytoff's analysis of "The Cultural Biography of Things: Commoditization as Process" in *The Social Life of Things: Commodities in Cultural Perspective*, ed. A. Appadurai (Cambridge: Cambridge University Press, 1986).

42 This raises the question of "authenticity." For interesting insights into the topic of authenticity, see Ames, *Cannibal Tours and Glass Boxes*, 73; Clifford, "Of Other Peoples," 121-30 and Dominguez, "Of Other Peoples" in *Dia Art Foundation Discussions*, 131-37; MacCannell, *The Tourist*; Daniel Miller, "Primitive Art and the Necessity of Primitivism to Art" in *The Myth of Primitivism*, 50-71; Signe Howell, "Art and Meaning" in *The Myth of Primitivism*, 215 37. An early and notable discussion of this topic is found in Walter Benjamin, "The Work of Art in the Age of Mechanical Reproduction" in *Illuminations*, ed. H. Arendt (New York: Schocken Books, 1969, first published 1936), 217-52.

43 See Marianna Torgovnick, *Gone Primitive: Savage Intellects, Modern Lives* (Chicago: University of Chicago Press, 1990) for a fascinating book on this topic.

44 Igor Kopytoff, "The Cultural Biography of Things"; Susan Stewart, *On Longing: Narratives of the Miniature, the Gigantic,* *the Souvenir, the Collection* (Baltimore: Johns Hopkins University Press, 1984); Renato Rosaldo, *Culture and Truth*, 68ff.; Nicholas Thomas, *Entangled Objects,* 10.

As Ruth Phillips puts it in relation to museum exhibitions, "Why Not Tourist Art" in *After Colonialism*, 30: "The flight of the rare art collector and the ethnologist from the commoditization and dislocation occurring in Western societies led them to make of the museum a shrine to the premodern that denied to Native Americans the representation of a modernity that had been imposed on them by force and then ingeniously negotiated under unavoidable conditions of colonial domination."

45 As Christina Toren puts it in "Leonardo's 'Last Supper' in Fiji" in *The Myth of Primitivism*, 263: "The extreme and indeed popular view, as represented by television documentaries and apparently well-meaning articles in the Sunday supplements, is that any appropriation of western culture by non-western peoples represents a 'loss' or a degeneration of the indigenous culture. The implicit assumption of western superiority is one that often escapes us—we see our own culture as 'enriched' by borrowings from others while the latter are inevitably 'undermined'."

46 Benjamin, "The Work of Art in the Age of Mechanical Reproduction" in *Illuminations*, 243.

47 Daniel Miller, "Primitive Art and the Necessity of Primitivism to Art" in *The Myth of Primitivism*, 62, discusses the authenticity imposed upon Native art by museums: "Often such claims to 'authenticity' are themselves based on the illusion that such societies did not change and were isolated prior to colonialism, allowing them to be characterised as 'pristine.' Alternatively objects are seen as authentic because they come from a society without internal division, in which each object is expressive of that society as a totality, or of an original spirituality true to itself and the materials it employs in representation."

48 Franz Boas, "The Decorative Art of the Indians of the North Pacific Coast," *Bulletin of the American Museum of*

Natural History 9 (1897):13 and *Primitive Art*, 212.

49 Bill Holm, "Will the Real Charles Edenshaw Please Stand Up?: The Problem of Attribution in Northwest Coast Indian Art" in *The World Is As Sharp As a Knife: An Anthology in Honour of Wilson Duff*, ed. Donald Abbott (Victoria: British Columbia Provincial Museum, 1981), 182.

50 Macnair, Hoover and Neary, *The Legacy*, 68, 70. See also Wilson Duff, "Charles Edenshaw: Master Artist" in *Arts of the Raven*; Alan Hoover, "Charles Edenshaw and the Creation of Human Beings," *American Indian Art* 8 (1983): 62-67; Susan Thomas, "The Life and Work of Charles Edenshaw: A Study of Innovation" (Master's thesis, University of British Columbia, 1967).

51 Boas, *Primitive Art*, 275, does, however, disregard as "fanciful" Edenshaw's explanation of the design on a box.

52 Holm, "Will the Real Charles Edenshaw Please Stand Up?" in *The World Is As Sharp As a Knife*, 197-99.

53 Holm, "Will the Real Charles Edenshaw Please Stand Up?" in *The World Is As Sharp As a Knife*, 176-77; Macnair, Hoover and Neary, *The Legacy*, 80. Bill Holm (personal communication to author, 1992) now believes that some of his 1981 Gwaytihl attributions are problematical. He notes that the British Museum documentation lists Simeon Stilthda as the carver of the Sphinx and feels that is probably accurate.

54 Holm, "Will the Real Charles Edenshaw Please Stand Up?" in *The World Is As Sharp As a Knife*, 190.

55 Jonaitis, "Franz Boas, John Swanton, and the New Haida Sculpture" and *A Wealth of Thought*.

56 For more on collecting, see Cole, *Captured Heritage*; Ira Jacknis, "Franz Boas and Exhibits" in *Objects and Others: Essays on Museums and Material Culture*, History of Anthropology 3, ed. G. Stocking Jr. (Madison: University of Wisconsin Press, 1985), 75-111; Jonaitis, *From the Land of the Totem Poles*.

57 Aldona Jonaitis and Richard Inglis, "Power, History and Authenticity: The Mowachaht Whaler's Washing Shrine," *South Atlantic Quarterly* 91 (1992):193-214; Jonaitis, "Franz Boas, John Swanton, and the New Haida Sculpture." This concept was first put forth by Frederic Jameson in *Postmodernism, or, The Cultural Logic of Late Capitalism*, in respect to an analysis of Frank Gehry's architecture. In contrast to some postmodernist theoreticians, wrapping does not dismiss the essence and reality of the artifact itself which always remain at the core.

58 Or, as Igor Kopytoff puts it in "The Cultural Biography of Things," one should investigate the "cultural biography of things" to understand how they are accepted, understood, and redefined. For another perspective on the manner in which representation transforms objects, see also Ames, *Cannibal Tours and Glass Boxes*, 139-50.

59 Kevin Robins, "Tradition and Translation: National Culture in Its Global Context" in *Enterprise and Heritage: Crosscurrents of National Culture*, eds. John Corner and Sylvia Harvey (London and New York: Routledge, 1991), 21-44.

60 Clifford, "Traveling Cultures" in *Cultural Studies*, 96-111. The concept of articulation, which analyses the "continual severing, realignment, and recombination" of cultural phenomena including art, can also be useful in this endeavour: Cary Nelson, Paula Treichler and Lawrence Grossberg, "Cultural Studies: An Introduction" in *Cultural Studies*, 8.

61 These terms follow Arjun Appadurai's useful classification of commodities, "Introduction: Commodities and the Politics of Value" in *The Social Life of Things: Commodities in Cultural Perspective*, ed. Arjun Appadurai (Cambridge: Cambridge University Press, 1986), 16.

62 Macnair, Hoover and Neary, *The Legacy*, 70.

63 Duff, *The Indian History of British Columbia*, 82.

64 Macnair, Hoover and Neary, *The Legacy*, 85.

65 Macnair and Hoover, *The Magic Leaves*, 190.

66 Sheehan, *Pipes That Won't Burn*, 119.

67 Macnair and Hoover, *The Magic Leaves*, 205-6; Drew and Wilson, *Argillite*.

68 Franz Boas, "The Development of the

Culture of Northwest America," *Science* XII (1888):195.

69 As Phillips ("Why Not Tourist Art" in *After Colonialism*, 31) puts it in relationship to Iroquois tourist art: "In many ways these souvenir items seem to be the most authentic representations of the courageous, innovative and creative adaptation that Woodlands aboriginal peoples made during one of the darkest periods of their history."

70 While other Northwest Coast artists have had one-person exhibits in museums such as the University of British Columbia Museum of Anthropology, Bill Reid's 1974 exhibition at the Vancouver Art Gallery was the first such show at an art museum.

71 Although raised in the white world, Bill Reid found among past Haida artists, especially Charles Edenshaw, a source of creativity that would inspire within him an astounding artistic mastery. See Karen Duffek, *Bill Reid: Beyond the Essential Form* (Vancouver: University of British Columbia Press, 1986); Doris Shadbolt, *Bill Reid* (Vancouver/Toronto: Douglas & McIntyre; Seattle: University of Washington Press, 1986); Joan Vastokas, "Bill Reid and the Native Renaissance" in *Stones, Bones and Skin: Ritual and Shamanic Art*, ed. Anne Brodzky et al. (Toronto: Society for Art Publications, 1977), 158-67.

72 The most noteworthy early exhibition on Northwest Coast art was *Arts of the Raven: Masterworks by the Northwest Coast Indian*, a 1967 exhibition at the Vancouver Art Gallery. The catalogue had essays by Wilson Duff, Bill Holm and Bill Reid.

73 Bill Holm, *Northwest Coast Indian Art: An Analysis of Form* (Seattle: University of Washington Press, 1965).

74 See Ames, *Cannibal Tours and Glass Boxes*, 59-60, for a suggestive analysis of how museum professionals contributed to the "renaissance" of Northwest Coast art that replaced this degenerate style with canonical creations.

75 The material in this section is based on interviews with Robert Davidson, conducted by the author in September 1992.

76 See Margaret B. Blackman, *During My Time: Florence Edenshaw Davidson, a Haida Woman* (Seattle: University of Washington Press; Vancouver/Toronto: Douglas & McIntyre, 1982) for an eloquent biography of Florence Edenshaw Davidson, Robert Davidson Sr.'s wife and Robert's grandmother.

77 Robert Davidson Sr. also carved boxes that Edenshaw painted and later worked with an artist named Ridley in the 1930s on a 15.2-m (50-foot) totem pole that stands in Jasper, Alberta.

78 Blackman, *During My Time*, 126-28, records Florence Edenshaw Davidson's words about painting this canoe and illustrates it.

79 According to Peter Macnair (personal communication to author, 1992), this book "had a profound effect on the Haida slate carvers of the time. Many of them, long established as argillite carvers, began to copy works from Barbeau, thus expanding their repertoires. Tim Pearson is a good example who is primarily a post 1950 carver although born ca. 1887."

80 See Drew and Wilson, *Argillite*, 117-21, for information on Pat McGuire.

81 Another commission reveals Davidson's deep sense of humour: when a dealer known for "having his hands all over the place in his collecting activities" asked for a bracelet, Davidson engraved on it an octopus.

82 See Ulli Steltzer, *A Haida Potlatch* (Vancouver/Toronto: Douglas & McIntyre; Seattle: University of Washington Press, 1984) for a photographic essay of this potlatch.

83 See Macnair, Hoover and Neary, *The Legacy*, 92, for an illustration of this house.

84 Not all Davidson's dances are appropriate to specific Haida ceremonies, and thus only certain masks are worn. For example, at a memorial sponsored by his grandmother's clan in Massett, he brought only the *Shark* masks because that was their crest.

85 Ames, *Cannibal Tours and Glass Boxes*, 82, poses several intriguing questions that Davidson's work addresses: "How does [this kind of art] fit into the life of the community to which the artist belongs? . . . To be considered indigenous, must a work of art be

derived from a recorded aesthetic tradition, and should that tradition still be 'living,' whatever that means?"

86 There is no question that the works of Bill Reid, Bill Holm and others contributed to a deeper understanding of the particular aesthetics of the nineteenth-century northern style, which had undergone a significant transformation during the twentieth century. There is also no question that the art market responded with vigour to these new old-style artworks.

87 This is not unlike the comment made in 1986 by Cherokee artist Jimmy Durham, quoted by Diana Nemiroff, "Modernism, Nationalism, and Beyond: A Critical History of Exhibitions of First Nations Art" in *Land Spirit Power: First Nations at the National Gallery of Canada*, eds. Diana Nemiroff, Robert Houle and Charlotte Townsend-Gault (Ottawa: National Gallery of Canada, 1992), 37: "Traditions exist and are guarded by Indian communities. One of the most important of these is dynamism. Constant change—adaptability, the inclusion of new ways and new material—is a tradition that our artists have particularly celebrated and have used to move and strengthen our societies."

Notes for "The Evolution of an Artist"

1 Joan Lowndes, "Contingencies: Ceremony, Alphabets, Spaces: Robert Davidson," *artscanada* 39 (November 1982):8.

2 Hilary Stewart, *Robert Davidson: Haida Printmaker* (Vancouver: Douglas & McIntyre, 1979), 15, describes Davidson's relationship with his father and grandfather. Davidson's relatives, in particular his grandmother Florence Edenshaw Davidson, have had a profound influence on his ideas.

3 Except where noted, all quotes from Robert Davidson in this essay are from a series of interviews between the author and Davidson in September, October and November 1992.

4 Robert Davidson, personal communication to the author, December 1992.

5 Stewart, *Robert Davidson*, 15.

6 Stewart, *Robert Davidson*, 17.

7 In 1966, Davidson was engaged to work carving argillite at Eaton's department store in downtown Vancouver. While Davidson was working, Reid introduced himself and invited the young carver to visit his studio. Davidson was aware of Reid's work but had not yet met the older artist. (Robert Davidson, personal communication to the author, December 1992.)

8 Stewart, *Robert Davidson*, 19.

9 Stewart, *Robert Davidson*, 17.

10 Stewart, *Robert Davidson*, 21.

11 Stewart, *Robert Davidson*, 40, notes that this is "the first design that he created entirely himself so as to convey a message visually."

Stewart's comments on all of Davidson's work reflect the artist's own ideas, which were conveyed to Stewart in conversation. (Robert Davidson, personal communication to the author, December 1992.)

12 In fact, Davidson made an error. The Bear is a Raven clan crest, and as an Eagle he did not have rights to it. That Davidson could make such an error is further indication of the lack of knowledge then in Massett about traditional culture. It is partially due to this fact that his pole raising served as a focus for the transmission of cultural knowledge amongst the Haida.

13 Robert Davidson in conversation with the author, November 1992.

14 Stewart, *Robert Davidson*, 8, identifies Ellen Neel as the first Northwest Coast Native artist to use screenprinting to reproduce designs.

15 Stewart, *Robert Davidson*, 47.

16 This totem pole is now permanently displayed in a small pavilion in the Dublin Zoo.

17 Lowndes, "Contingencies," 4.

18 Stewart, *Robert Davidson*, 56.

19 Stewart, *Robert Davidson*, 63.

20 Ibid.

21 Stewart, *Robert Davidson*, 65. The child is depicted as a Raven because in Haida culture the child is a member of the mother's clan.

22 Robert Davidson, personal communication to the author, 30 November 1992.

23 Lowndes, "Contingencies," 6.

24 Ibid.

25 Alan Hoover, "Innovation in Contemporary Haida Art: The Bracelets of Robert Davidson" (Paper delivered at the eighth biennial conference of the Native American Art Studies Association, Sioux Falls, South Dakota, September 1991), no pagination.

26 Hoover, "Innovation," no pagination.

27 Ibid.

28 Peter Macnair, Alan Hoover and Kevin Neary, *The Legacy: Continuing Traditions of Canadian Northwest Coast Indian Art* (Victoria: British Columbia Provincial Museum, 1980), 89-90, note that "An important feature of Davidson's personal style is the 'soft' ovoid which forms the eye [of the *Whale* bracelet]. It is convex on the bottom, contrary to the traditional rule. Edenshaw was successful in rendering ovoids in this way. Only these two are truly effective with this form."

29 Ibid.

30 Ibid.

31 Robert Davidson, personal communication to the author, October 1992.

32 Ibid.

33 Ibid.

34 Macnair, Hoover and Neary, *The Legacy*, 88.

35 Stewart, *Robert Davidson*, 78 and 81.

36 Stewart, *Robert Davidson*, 85, notes that Davidson used the circle extensively from this point on.

37 Ibid.

38 Stewart, *Robert Davidson*, 109, points out that Davidson did a three-colour (red, black, blue-green) print in 1975, using the blue-green as the primary formline for the image. He did not release the print.

39 Ibid.

40 Stewart, *Robert Davidson*, 91.

41 Lowndes, "Contingencies," 4.

42 Stewart, *Robert Davidson*, 90.

43 Lowndes, "Contingencies," 4.

44 Stewart, *Robert Davidson*, 93.

45 Lowndes, "Contingencies," 4; Hoover, "Innovation," no pagination.

46 Stewart, *Robert Davidson*, 105.

47 Robert Davidson, personal communication to the author, February 1993.

48 Lowndes, "Contingencies," 6.

49 Ibid.

50 Robert Davidson, personal communication to the author, February 1993.

51 Davidson as quoted by Lowndes, "Contingencies."

52 Lowndes, "Contingencies," 8.

53 Stewart, *Robert Davidson*, 92.

54 Davidson as quoted by Marjorie Halpin in *Cycles: The Graphic Art of Robert Davidson, Haida*, Museum note no. 7 (Vancouver: University of British Columbia Museum of Anthropology, 1979), 10.

55 "Tribute to the Living Haida," a four-day celebration, was very important for Davidson. It allowed him to assert his conviction that Haida art and culture should not dwell in the past; in order for living people to succeed, they had to move beyond the past, taking what was important and valuable but adapting these things to life now. Davidson has pointed out that the names of his potlatches have been very deliberately chosen. (Robert Davidson, personal communication to the author, December 1992.)

56 Davidson's first marriage ended in 1977. He met Dorothy Grant in 1979, and they were married in 1986. Their collaboration, with Davidson providing the designs and Grant making the garments, continues to the present. Dorothy Grant founded a successful fashion design firm, Feastwear, and Davidson has provided many of the designs applied to the clothing—dresses, jackets and so on—for sale to non-Haida people.

57 Lowndes, "Contingencies," 8, provides

more information on this traumatic incident.

58 The panels and housefront for the Edenshaw Memorial Longhouse were all conceived of in sculptural terms. Davidson's only previous flat painting experience was in 1969, painting designs for a mural at the entrance to the exhibition *Masterpieces of Indian and Eskimo Art from Canada* at the National Gallery of Canada in Ottawa, Ontario.

Davidson has said (personal communication to the author, December 1992) that he found the experience unsatisfactory due to the fact that he was terribly rushed. He had only eight days to produce four oversize figures of Raven, Eagle, Hawk and Thunderbird. This forced him to change only the heads and repeat the bodies. In 1983, he painted his second wall mural for the Southwest Museum in Los Angeles.

59 Both Davidson and the dealer Bud Mintz commented that collectors of prints were reluctant to commit themselves to works of this scale and this departure from iconographic orthodoxy (personal communications to the author, October/November 1992).

60 Davidson and Ulli Steltzer, who has photographed all of his poles, are planning a volume devoted exclusively to his poles and their creation. Therefore, his poles are not dealt with extensively here.

61 Robert Davidson, personal communication to the author, November 1992.

62 Robert Davidson, "Haida Idea or Haida Ideal?" (Paper, unpublished, 1986) on the work of Bill Reid.

63 Robert Davidson, personal communication to the author, October 1992.

64 Robert Davidson as quoted by Charlotte Townsend-Gault in Diana Nemiroff, Robert Houle and Charlotte Townsend-Gault, *Land Spirit Power: First Nations at the National Gallery of Canada* (Ottawa: National Gallery of Canada, 1992), 136.

65 These images were published as prints in 1987.

66 The *Eagle Spirit* mask, Davidson's second version of the subject, recalls one described by Lowndes, "Contingincies," 8: "The mask is all red, drenched in the blood of a strenuous re-birth. It has a terrible imperiousness as it fixes you with its brass eyes like the gaze of the mature Eagle. Its beak hooks over a human mouth set with clenched teeth (operculum shell). Shaggy eyebrows of goat's hair quiver with every movement as do the eagle feathers set in the top."

Peter Macnair, "Robert Davidson: Walking the Knife Edge," in *Robert Davidson: "A Voice from the Inside"* (Vancouver: Derek Simpkins Gallery of Tribal Art, 1992), 15, notes that one of the Eagles appears to have three wings.

Breaking the Totem Barrier is a totem pole fully in the round. Davidson conceived of the pole as encouraging the viewer to walk around it. (In order to prevent the pole from cracking, the centre was hollowed out.)

Davidson addressed a similar problem in the exceptional *Dorsal Fin*. Through the device of the elongated fingers of the human figures, which bend around the fin, Davidson realizes a fully rounded figure.

67 Macnair, "Robert Davidson," 15.

68 Robert Davidson, artist's statement in *Robert Davidson: An Exhibition of Northwest Coast Art* (Vancouver: Inuit Gallery of Vancouver Ltd., 1989), no pagination.

69 Robert Davidson, "The World Is As Sharp As the Edge of a Knife," artist's statement in *Robert Davidson: "A Voice from the Inside"* (Vancouver: Derek Simpkins Gallery of Tribal Art, 1992), 8.

70 Ibid.

CHRONOLOGY

1946
Born Robert Charles Davidson on 4
November, in his mother's home village of
Hydaburg, Alaska. Second child of Claude
and Vivian Davidson, and great-grandson of
the legendary Haida artist Charles
Edenshaw.

1947
Family moves to father's home village, Old
Massett, on Haida Gwaii (the Queen
Charlotte Islands, off the coast of northern
British Columbia).

1959
Begins carving argillite under the tutelage of
his father and his paternal grandfather,
Robert Davidson Sr.

1965
Moves to Vancouver, British Columbia, to
complete high school. Studies Haida art in
local museum collections. Learns the
rudiments of silkscreen printing at Point
Grey Secondary School.

1966
Meets Bill Reid and begins an eighteen-
month apprenticeship with him, learning
Haida design principles as well as gold and
silver engraving; they carve a small pole
together.

1967–68
Studies design, painting, pottery and
sculpture at the Vancouver School of Art.
Meets anthropologists Wilson Duff and Bill
Holm.

1968
Teaches carving at the Gitanmaax School of
Northwest Coast Indian Art in 'Ksan,

northern British Columbia. Makes his first
silkscreen print, using a Haida design.
    Meets archaeologist/curator Susan
Thomas.

1969
Marries Susan Thomas; announces the
marriage with an original silkscreen print.
    Carves and erects the 12.2-m (40-foot)
Bear Mother totem pole in Massett, the first
pole to be raised in Haida Gwaii in nearly
fifty years. Celebrates the pole raising with a
potlatch, reviving ceremonial traditions.
Carves a dance screen, designs button
blankets.
    Commissioned by the National Gallery
of Canada in Ottawa to paint a mural for the
entrance to an exhibition, *Masterpieces of
Indian and Eskimo Art from Canada*.

1970
Under the sponsorship of the University of
British Columbia Museum of Anthropology,
demonstrates carving in Montreal at Man
and His World (a continuation of Expo '67,
which in 1970 had as its theme Canada's
indigenous peoples), and presents the
resulting 3-m (10-foot) pole to the City of
Montreal.
    Chosen as the Canadian delegate to the
World Council of Craftsmen conference in
Dublin, Ireland. Carves a 3-m (10-foot) pole
and presents it to the Republic of Ireland,
which cedes it to the City of Dublin.

1971
First solo exhibition, in the gift shop of the
Centennial Museum (now the Vancouver
Museum) in Vancouver. The show quickly
sells out.
    Moves to Whonnock near Vancouver,
where he builds a studio. Designs and prints

announcements of the solo exhibition and the move.

1972
Demonstrates Haida carving in Bern, Switzerland. Studies Northwest Coast art in museums and private collections in Switzerland and Germany.

Death of his mother, Vivian, by drowning; one year later, creates a memorial print using a double-headed Eagle design.

1973
Birth of his daughter, Sara; designs and prints an original birth announcement.

Expands his Whonnock studio and collaborates with Bill Reid in carving a 3.7-m (12-foot) pole for Walter Koerner.

Hand adzes massive roof beams for a Haida longhouse at the British Columbia Provincial Museum (now the Royal British Columbia Museum) in Victoria, B.C.

1974–75
Undertakes numerous private jewelry and carving commissions. Continues to develop proficiency in silkscreen printing techniques and to invent and innovate within Haida design traditions.

1976
Birth of his son Benjamin; creates a family theme print.

Commissioned by the Canadian Broadcasting Corporation to make a carved screen for the B.C. Director's office in its complex on Hamilton Street in Vancouver. Employs a circular sea monster design on laminated red cedar.

Commissioned by North West Cultural Society to design a Haida coin for its Indian Heritage series.

1976–77
Assists Bill Reid in carving a 12.2-m (40-foot) frontal pole for the Skidegate Band Council offices on Haida Gwaii.

1977
Founding member of Northwest Coast Indian Artists Guild, which holds its first print show in October at the Vancouver Art Gallery shop.

Builds Shark House carving shed at

Massett in order to execute a monument to Charles Edenshaw commissioned by Parks Canada. Designs, carves and paints the housefront for the Charles Edenshaw Memorial Longhouse at Massett.

First marriage ends.

1978
Carves four 4-m (13-foot) interior house posts for the Charles Edenshaw Memorial Longhouse; organizes and oversees an apprenticeship program for eight young Haida artists.

Dedication of the Edenshaw memorial, with a commemorating potlatch. Designs cover for the dedication program.

1979
First retrospective print exhibition, *Cycles: The Graphic Art of Robert Davidson*, held at the University of British Columbia Museum of Anthropology in Vancouver.

Publication of Hilary Stewart's book, *Robert Davidson: Haida Printmaker*.

Meets Haida artist/designer Dorothy Grant.

1980
Begins collaborating with Dorothy Grant in the design of ceremonial garments such as button blankets and dance aprons.

Organizes and sponsors a four-day potlatch celebration, "Tribute to the Living Haida," in Massett.

Forms a group, the Rainbow Creek Dancers, to perform traditional and contemporary Haida songs and dances.

1981
Organizes and sponsors "Children of the Good People" potlatch in Massett. Adopts Nuu-chah-nulth artist Joe David as his brother and bestows a Haida name upon him.

Fire destroys the Charles Edenshaw Memorial Longhouse.

1981–82
Continues to exhibit locally and abroad. Executes private commissions.

1983
Creates a mural for the Southwest Museum in Los Angeles.

1984
Carves *The Three Watchmen,* a three-pole commission for the Maclean-Hunter building at College Park in Toronto.

Commissioned by the Catholic Church of Vancouver to make an Eagle talking stick for presentation to Pope John Paul II during a papal visit to Vancouver.

Teaches an advanced course in Northwest Coast totem pole design at Ketchikan, Alaska.

Large *Frog* in bronze commissioned by PepsiCo, to be installed at its International Sculpture Park in Purchase, New York. Before being shipped to Purchase, *Frog* is exhibited at the Vancouver Art Gallery (spring 1985).

1984–86
Executes and exhibits a sculpture commission, *Raven Bringing Light to the World* for the National Museum of Man (now the Canadian Museum of Civilization) in Hull, Quebec. Bronze casting and gilding funded by Marmie Hess of Calgary. The work is unveiled at the University of British Columbia Museum of Anthropology in Vancouver and shown at the Expo 86 Canada Pavilion in Vancouver, the Glenbow Museum in Calgary and the McMichael Canadian Collection in Kleinburg, before permanent installation in Hull.

1986
Watercolour painting reproduced as Expo 86 poster.

Three-pole grouping, *Three Variations of Killer Whale Myth*, commissioned by PepsiCo and installed at its International Sculpture Park in Purchase, New York.

Moves home from Whonnock to Surrey, near Vancouver.

Builds studio/carving shed at Semiahmoo Village on the Salish Reserve in White Rock, B.C.

Marries Dorothy Grant.

1987–88
Begins collaborating with Dorothy Grant in appliqué designs for her line of nonceremonial clothing.

1989
Undertakes a private commission, *Skeleton Housefront*, which includes a 15.2-m (50-foot) pole, roof beams and two flanking Watchmen figures, in Toronto.

Carves a 6.1-m (20-foot) pole, *Breaking the Totem Barrier*, for a private collector in New York.

Stages a two-day feast, "Every Year the Salmon Come Back," in Massett.

1990
Gives a multimedia performance at Grouse Mountain, B.C.

Begins a privately commissioned 5.2-m (17-foot) pole, *The Inside Job*, in West Vancouver, B.C.

Exhibits in solo and group shows in Bellingham, Washington, and San Francisco.

1992
Awarded an Honorary Doctorate in Fine Arts by the University of Victoria, Victoria, B.C.

Solo exhibitions in Philadelphia and Vancouver, B.C.

1993
Major retrospective exhibition at the Vancouver Art Gallery.

SOLO EXHIBITIONS

1971
Robert Davidson, Centennial Museum Shop, Vancouver, B.C.

1978
Robert Davidson, The Bent Box Gallery, Vancouver, B.C.

1979
Cycles: The Graphic Art of Robert Davidson, University of British Columbia Museum of Anthropology, Vancouver, B.C.

1983
Robert Davidson, Faschwerk Gallery, Bad Salzuflen, Federal Republic of Germany.

Robert Davidson Paintings, Maple Ridge Gallery, Maple Ridge, B.C.

1985
Frog (unveiling of PepsiCo sculpture commission), Vancouver Art Gallery, Vancouver, B.C.

1986
Raven Bringing Light to the World (unveiling of Canadian Museum of Civilization sculpture commission) at the University of British Columbia Museum of Anthropology, Vancouver, B.C. (See Chronology for exhibition itinerary.)

1989
Robert Davidson, Inuit Gallery, Vancouver, B.C.

Eagle Song, Derek Simpkins Gallery of Tribal Art, Vancouver, B.C.

1990
Robert Davidson, Whatcom County Museum, Bellingham, Washington.

1992
Robert Davidson: Contemporary Forms, Art Space Gallery, Philadelphia.

Robert Davidson: Recollections, Arthur Ross Gallery, University of Pennsylvania, Philadelphia.

A Voice from the Inside, Derek Simpkins Gallery of Tribal Art, Vancouver, B.C.

1993
Robert Davidson: Eagle of the Dawn, Vancouver Art Gallery, Vancouver, B.C.

GROUP EXHIBITIONS

1967
Arts of the Raven, Vancouver Art Gallery, Vancouver, B.C.

1971
The Legacy, British Columbia Provincial Museum, Victoria, B.C. Exhibition travelled to museums and galleries across Canada during the 1970s; an expanded version appeared at the Edinburgh Festival in 1980 and at the University of British Columbia Museum of Anthropology, Vancouver, B.C., in 1981.

1977
Northwest Coast Indian Artists Guild, Vancouver Art Gallery Shop, Vancouver, B.C.

1978

Untitled Group Exhibition of Prints (Robert Davidson, Norman Tait and Joe David),

The Bent Box Gallery, Vancouver, B.C. *Northwest Coast Indian Artists Guild—1978 Graphics Collection*, University of British Columbia Museum of Anthropology, Vancouver, B.C.

1979

Donnervogel und Raubwal: Die Indianische Kunst der Nordwestkuste Nordamericas, Museum fur Volkerkunde und Christians Verlag, Hamburg, Federal Republic of Germany.

Wood, Metal and Paper, Heard Museum, Phoenix, Arizona.

1980

Group Exhibition, American Indian Community House Gallery, New York.

Northwest Renaissance, Burnaby Art Gallery, Burnaby, B.C.

1981

Pipes That Won't Smoke, Coal That Won't Burn: Haida Sculpture in Argillite, Glenbow Museum, Calgary, Alberta.

1983

Vancouver: Art and Artists 1931-1983, Vancouver Art Gallery, Vancouver, B.C.

British Columbia Printmakers, Art Gallery of Greater Victoria, Victoria, B.C.

1985

The Northwest Coast Native Print, Art Gallery of Greater Victoria, Victoria, B.C.

1986

Lost and Found Traditions, organized by the American Federation of Arts, opened at the American Museum of Natural History, New York, and toured throughout the United States of America, 1986–1989. (At tour's end, the collection was donated to the Los Angeles County Museum, Los Angeles.)

1987

Profiles of Heritage: Images of Wildlife by British Columbia Artists, organized by the Centennial Wildlife Society of British Columbia, initially exhibited at the Art Gallery of Greater Victoria, Victoria, B.C., and toured throughout British Columbia.

Hands of Creation, Inuit Gallery, Vancouver, B.C.

Recent Acquisitions, Vancouver Art Gallery, Vancouver, B.C.

1988

In the Shadow of the Sun: Contemporary Indian and Inuit Art in Canada, organized by the Canadian Museum of Civilization, Hull, Quebec. Opened as *Zeitgenossische Kunst der Indianer und Eskimos in Kanada* at Museum am Ostwall and Museum fur Kunst und Kulturgeschichte, Dortmund, Federal Republic of Germany. Travelled to Canadian Museum of Civilization, Hull, Art Gallery of Nova Scotia, Halifax, and Rijtsmuseum Voor Volkenkunde, Leiden, The Netherlands.

1989

The Northwest: A Collector's Vision, Barrie Art Gallery, Barrie, Ontario.

Masks, Inuit Gallery, Vancouver, B.C.

Beyond the Revival, Charles H. Scott Gallery, Vancouver, B.C.

1990

Haida Ritual Art: The Insistent Present, Meridian Gallery, San Francisco.

Visions for the Wilderness, Stein Valley Festival, Mount Currie, B.C.

1992

Land Spirit Power: First Nations at the National Gallery of Canada, National Gallery of Canada, Ottawa, Ontario.

172

Abbot, Donald N., ed. *The World Is As Sharp As a Knife: An Anthology in Honour of Wilson Duff*. Victoria: British Columbia Provincial Museum, 1981.

Appelbe, Alison. "Haida Artist Robert Davidson: Helping to Legitimize Northwest Coast Art." *Western Living*, April 1979, 9–11.

"Art Lover Helps Fill Tall Order for Office Tower." *Financial Post* 78 (15 September 1984), 19.

Ashwell, Reg. "The Haida Art of Robert Davidson and Bill Reid." *Arts West* 3 (January 1978): 33–36; (April 1978): 39–43.

————. "Northwest Coast: A Gathering." *Arts West* 4 (January–February 1979): 34–37.

Beker, Marilyn. "Young craftsman makes wood live in the tradition of his ancestors." *Montreal Gazette*, 22 August 1970, 9.

"Beyond Tradition." *Vancouver Sun*, 11 March 1983, E3.

Blackman, Margaret B., and Edwin S. Hall. "Contemporary Northwest Coast Indian Art: Tradition and Innovation in Serigraphy." *American Indian Art* 10 (Summer 1981):24–37.

Bloore, Ronald L. "In the Mainstream . . ." *artscanada* 38 (March 1982):118–22.

Boyco, Eugene. *This Was the Time*. 16-mm film, 16 min. Ottawa: National Film Board, 1970.

Brissenden, Constance. "The Eagle Soars." *Western Living*, March 1990, 63–69.

Carter, Anthony. "At Haida: A New Totem." *Beautiful British Columbia*, Fall 1970, 34–35.

Charles, Sharon. "Voice from the Inside." *Semiahmoo Sounder*, 7:6 (June 1992), 32–35.

Coe, Ralph T. *Lost and Found Traditions: Native American Art 1965–1985*. New York: University of Washington Press in association with the American Federation of the Arts, 1986.

Davidson, Robert. Remarks at opening of exhibition *Images Stone B.C.*, Vancouver Art Gallery, 6 May 1975.

————. "Three Sides to a Coin: A Haida Viewpoint." *Canadian Conservation Institute* 3 (1978):10–12.

Davison, Liane. *Profiles of a Heritage: Images of Wildlife by British Columbia Artists*. Victoria: Centennial Wildlife Society of British Columbia, 1987.

Dawn, Leslie. *The Northwest Coast Native Print: A Contemporary Tradition Comes of Age*. Victoria: Art Gallery of Greater Victoria, 1984.

DeMott, Barbara, and Maureen Milburn. *Beyond the Revival: Contemporary North West Native Art*. Vancouver: Charles Scott Gallery, 1989.

Deragisch, Ricky. *Tools and Materials*. Videorecording, 15 min. The Big A Series. Lincoln, Nebraska: GPN, 1987.

Dickason, Olive Patricia. *Indian Arts in Canada*. Ottawa: Department of Indian and Northern Affairs, 1972.

Dikeakos, Christos. *Adding more words to the dictionary: an appreciation of Robert Davidson's "Recent Painting" exhibition, Maple Ridge Gallery, February 22 to March 18, 1983*. Maple Ridge, B.C.: Maple Ridge Art Gallery, 1983.

Drew, Leslie. *Haida, Their Art and Culture*. Surrey, B.C.: Hancock House, 1982.

Drew, Leslie, and Douglas Wilson. *Argillite: Art of the Haida*. North Vancouver, B.C.: Hancock House, 1980.

Duff, Wilson. *Arts of the Raven: Masterworks by the Northwest Coast Indian*. Vancouver: Vancouver Art Gallery, 1967.

Duffek, Karen. "The Revival of Northwest Coast Indian Art. In *Vancouver: Art and Artists 1931–1983*, 312–17. Vancouver: Vancouver Art Gallery, 1983.

The Far Land. 16-mm film, 30 min. Klahanee Film Series. Vancouver: Canadian Broadcasting Corporation, 1969.

Fitterman, Lisa. "Taking Hold of the Reins." *Vancouver Sun*, 21 November 1992, E9.

Flanders, John. *Craftsman's Way: Canadian Expressions*. Toronto: University of Toronto Press, 1981.

Gilbert, Richard. *Haida Carver*. 16-mm film, 12 min. Ottawa: National Film Board, 1964.

Glavin, Terry. "Noblest Eagle of Them All." *Vancouver Sun*, 9 May 1988, B1, B6.

Godley, Elizabeth. "Haida Artist Pushes Boundaries." *Vancouver Sun*, 19 April 1989, C6.

Haberland, Wolfgang. *Donnervogel und Raubwal: Die Indianische Kunst der Nordwestkuste Nordamericas*. Hamburg: Museum fur Volkerkunde und Christians Verlag, 1979.

"Haida Artist Has Anxious Moments." *Halifax Chronicle Herald*, 14 April 1989, E7.

Hall Jr., Edwin S., Margaret B. Blackman and Vincent Rickard. *Northwest Coast Indian Graphics, an Introduction to Silkscreen Prints*. Seattle: University of Washington Press; Vancouver/Toronto: Douglas & McIntyre, 1981.

Halpin, Marjorie. "Beyond Nostalgia: The Graphic Art of Robert Davidson." *Vanguard* 8 (November 1979):6.

————. *Cycles: The Graphic Art of Robert Davidson, Haida*. Museum note no. 7. Vancouver: University of British Columbia Museum of Anthropology, 1979.

————. *Totem Poles: An Illustrated Guide*. Museum Note no. 13. Vancouver: University of British Columbia Press in association with the University of British Columbia Museum of Anthropology, 1981.

Hands of Creation: An Exhibition of North West Coast Native Art. Vancouver: Inuit Gallery, 1987.

Hargittay, Clara. "Robert Davidson: Maclean Hunter Building." *Vanguard* 13 (October 1984): 32.

Herem, Barry "Robert Davidson Totems are Installed at PepsiCo Sculpture Garden, N.Y." *Northwest Arts* 12 (24 October 1986), 3.

Hoffman, Gerhard, ed. *Zeitgenossische Kunst der Indianer und Eskimos in Kanada*. Edition Cantz, 1988.

Hopkins, Thomas. "The Happy Rebirth of an Intricate Art." *Maclean's*, 14 April 1980, 56–58.

Hunter, Don. "Master Carver Breaks Ground." *Vancouver Province*, 15 June 1986, 18.

Isaac, Tim. "Haida Carver Defines Culture." *Kahtou* 8 (19 February 1990), 15–17.

Jensen, Doreen, and Polly Sargent. *Robes of*

Power: Totem Poles on Cloth. Museum note no. 17. Vancouver: University of British Columbia Press, 1986.

Johnson, Eve. "An Art Reborn." *Vancouver Sun*, 25 October 1986, C1–C2.

Jonaitis, Aldona. *From the Land of the Totem Poles: The Northwest Coast Indian Art Collection at the American Museum of Natural History*. Seattle: University of Washington Press in association with the American Museum of Natural History; Vancouver/Toronto: Douglas & McIntyre, 1988.

Laurence, Robin. "From Revival to Innovation." *Georgia Straight*, 11–18 August 1989, 19–20.

————. "Renewing the Culture of Ceremony." *Georgia Straight,* 4–11 December 1992, 33.

Lowndes, Joan. "Confidence of a master." *Vancouver Sun*, 18 November 1976, 31.

————. "Contingencies: Ceremony, Alphabets, Spaces: Robert Davidson." *artscanada* 39 (November 1982):2–9.

————. "Joan Lowndes talks to the carver." *Vancouver Sun*, 19 February 1971, 8A.

Macnair, Peter L. "Inheritance and Innovation: Northwest Coast Artists Today." *artscanada* 30 (December 1973/January 1974):182–89.

Macnair, Peter L., Alan L. Hoover and Kevin Neary. *The Legacy: Tradition and Innovation in Northwest Coast Indian Art*. Vancouver/Toronto: Douglas & McIntyre; Seattle: University of Washington Press, 1984.

Mayhew, Anne. "Return of the Salmon Eaters." *Beautiful British Columbia*, Fall 1990, 34–45.

Moore, William. *The Northwest, a Collector's Vision: An Exhibition of Native Art of the Pacific Northwest Coast from the Peacock Collection*. Barrie, Ontario: Barrie Art Gallery, 1988.

Murphy, Maureen. "The Talking Stick." *B.C. Catholic*, 7 October 1984, 18.

Nahanee, Maurice. "Three Haida Totems Destined for New York." *Kahtou* 4 (August 1986), 13.

Nemiroff, Diana, Robert Houle and Charlotte Townsend-Gault. *Land Spirit Power: First Nations at the National Gallery of Canada*. Ottawa: National Gallery of Canada, 1992.

The Northwest Coast Native Print. Victoria: Art Gallery of Greater Victoria, 1985.

Perry, Art. "West Coast Prints: For Soul or For Sale?" *Province*, 22 November 1979, D1.

Persons, Heather. "Indian Art." *Westworld*, January–February 1975, 31.

Philpott, Joanne. "Carving a Niche in Two Worlds." *Globe & Mail*, 14 September 1984, 14.

Printmaking in British Columbia 1889–1983. Victoria: Art Gallery of Greater Victoria, 1983.

The Revival. Videorecording, 30 min. Victoria: British Columbia Ministry of Education, 1982.

"Robert Davidson." *Tawow* 2 (Summer 1971), 28–31.

Robert Davidson: An Exhibition of Northwest Coast Native Art. Vancouver: Inuit Gallery of Vancouver, 1989.

Robert Davidson, Exhibition: "A Voice from the Inside." Vancouver: Derek Simpkins Gallery of Tribal Art, 1992.

Rosenberg, Ann. "Amble in World of Wonders." *Vancouver Sun*, 21 November 1992, C9.

Roxborough, Bill, and Michael Brodie. *The*

Three Watchmen. Videorecording, 27 min. Toronto: College Park, 1986.

Scott, Andrew. "A Culture Brought Back to Life." *Vancouver Sun*, 16 November 1979, 6L.

Sheehan, Carol. *Eye of the Dreamer: Heroes and Heroic Transformation in the Northwest Coast Silkscreen Prints from the Collection of the National Museum of Man*. Thunder Bay, Ontario: Thunder Bay Native Exhibition Centre and Centre for Indian Art, 1985.

————. *Pipes That Won't Smoke, Coal That Won't Burn: Haida Sculpture in Argillite*. Calgary, Alberta: Glenbow Museum, 1981.

Shein, Brian. "High Rise Totems." *Equinox,* March, 116–17.

Spotswood, Ken. "Talented Haida Widening Field." *Province*, 20 November 1970, 6.

Steltzer, Ulli. *A Haida Potlatch*. Vancouver/Toronto: Douglas & McIntyre; Seattle: University of Washington Press, 1984.

————. *Indian Artists at Work*. Vancouver: J. J. Douglas, 1976.

Stewart, Hilary. *Looking at Indian Art of the Northwest Coast*. Vancouver: Douglas & McIntyre; Seattle: University of Washington Press, 1979.

————. *Robert Davidson: Haida Printmaker*. Vancouver: Douglas & McIntyre, 1979.

————. *Totem Poles*. Vancouver/ Toronto: Douglas & McIntyre; Seattle: University of Washington Press, 1990.

Townsend-Gault, Charlotte. "Having Voices and Using Them." *Arts Magazine* 65 (February 1991), 65–70.

Watmough, David. "Past and Future Meld in Museum's *Legacy*." *Vancouver Province* , 7 March 1982, magazine, 5.

Wood World (Council of the Forest Industries of British Columbia, Vancouver), second quarter 1973, 18–20.

Yaa-7aa-Me—I'm in Awe. Videorecording, 24 min. Richmond, B.C.: Matrix Video Services, 1981. Distributed by Image Media Services Ltd.

"You Can Still Tell a Man by His Hands." *Maclean's*, December 1971, 29–37.

Young, David. *Northwest Renaissance*. Burnaby, B.C.: Burnaby Art Gallery, 1980.

INDEX